The Consulting Supervisor's Workbook
Supporting New Supervisors

Linda A. LeBlanc
LeBlanc Behavioral Consulting

and

Tyra P. Sellers
TP Sellers, LLC

© 2022 KeyPress Publishing
930 South Harbor City Blvd., Melbourne, FL 32901

Copyright © 2022 by KeyPress Publishing

Authors: Linda LeBlanc & Tyra Sellers

The Consulting Supervisor's Workbook: Supporting New Supervisors

Published by: KeyPress Publishing
Cover design: Jana Burtner
Text design: Jana Burtner
Illustration: Jana Burtner
Production Coordinator: Shauna Costello

All rights reserved. No part of this publication may be reproduced, stored in a retrieval system, or transmitted in any form or by any means, electronic, mechanical, photocopying, recording, or otherwise without the prior permission of the publisher or in accordance with the provisions of the Copyright, Designs and Patents Act 1988 or under the terms of any license permitting limited copying issued by the Copyright Licensing Agency.

ISBN 978-1-7377574-3-6

Distributed by:
ABA Technologies, Inc.
930 South Harbor City Blvd, Suite 402
Melbourne, FL 32901
Telephone: 321-222-6822
www.abatechnologies.com

KeyPress Publishing books are available at a special discount for bulk purchases by corporations, institutions, and other organizations. For more information, please call 321-222-6822 or email keypress@abatechnologies.com.

Acknowledgments

We would like to acknowledge Scott LaPorta, Erin O'Brien, Janet Lund, Francine Holguin, Dana Meller, Jayme Mews, Audrey Hoffman and Kristine Rodriguez, who reviewed early drafts of the book and provided invaluable feedback.

Contents

I. **Introduction**   6

II. **Getting Ready**   10

III. **Month to Month Guides:**   27

    a. Month 1 29

    b. Month 2 41

    c. Month 3 51

IV. **Month-to-Month Guides**   59

    a. Month 4 60

    b. Month 5 62

    c. Month 6 64

    d. Month 7 66

    e. Month 8 68

    f. Month 9 73

    g. Month 10 76

    h. Month 11 78

    i. Month 12 80

V. **Specific Skills**   83

    a. Compassionate Care and Therapeutic Relationships 85

    b. Enhancing Learning:
        Self-Monitoring, Describing, and Asking Meaningful Questions 89

    c. Evaluating Effects of Supervision 93

    d. Feedback and Difficult Conversations 97

    e. Ongoing Monitoring and Performance Management 102

    f. Organization and Time Management..........................106

    g. Problem-Solving and Decision Making........................110

    h. Public Speaking and Professional Presentations..............116

    i. Scope Of Competence..121

    j. Self-Care..125

    k. Teaching Effectively Using BST.............................128

VI. References   132

Introduction

On January 1, 2022, the Behavior Analyst Certification Board® (BACB®, 2021) instituted a requirement for oversight of the supervisory efforts of newly certified Board Certified Behavior Analysts® (BCBAs®). Any BCBA providing supervision to trainees accruing fieldwork experience toward certification in their first-year post certification must have oversight of that supervision by a Consulting Supervisor (CS). The BCBA and their qualified CS must meet every month for guidance on effective supervision practices (BACB, 2021). The CS, in this case you, must have been a BCBA for at least five years and be in good standing with respect to their certification, supervision training, and ongoing CE requirements. Although the term used by the BACB to refer to your role is CS, you are also in a position to serve as a mentor to the new BCBAs with whom you work. The term mentor refers to someone who is a positive, guiding influence in another person's life with accrued life and professional experience that informs the guidance they provide (LeBlanc, Sellers et al., 2020).

Based on the steep growth trajectory in our profession, the percentage of BCBAs considered new (i.e., certified in the last 5 years) will continue to become an ever greater majority of all BCBAs. This means that there will be a limited pool of qualified CSs to provide the necessary support for those newly certified BCBAs. You and your services will be in high demand! This new requirement also presents a tremendous opportunity for the profession to fully embrace the value and power of meaningful and effective supervision as laid out by LeBlanc, Sellers et al. (2020). Those newly certified behavior analysts will have support and guidance to help them fully realize their valuable role as a supervisor. More senior behavior analysts like you have the opportunity to continue to grow in their professional roles by becoming a consultant and a mentor to their junior colleagues.

The BACB also provides general guidance about the structure of the consultation you will be providing (BACB, 2021). For example, the New Supervisor (NS) must meet with their CS for at least one hour per month until the NS has been certified for at least one year. The consultation meeting must be synchronous and one-on-one (online meetings are permitted). The purpose of consultation is to provide the NS with guidance and professional development for facilitating high-quality supervision of trainees (BACB, 2021). That is, the function of the CS under this requirement is NOT to provide ongoing supervision related to the general practice (e.g., caseload management activities with clients) of your newly certified BCBAs during this protected hour per month. Of course, new BCBAs should be receiving clinical support and oversight at other times from you or from others, but that support should not usurp your focused consultation on supervisory practices.

The focus of the consultation should be supervision, training, and performance management. The consultation should focus on the formal requirements (e.g., understanding the fieldwork standards, designing a contract), as well as on the strategies used to supervise and the curriculum used when supervising, among other topics and skills. The overarching purpose of your efforts as CS is to convey to your NSs what you do as a supervisor for others and why it is important for the NS to do the same things with their supervisees (e.g., RBT®s, BCaBA®s) and trainees pursuing fieldwork experience. Most people qualified to serve as a CS will likely have been providing case consultation and oversight for other BCBAs or overseeing the clinical work of trainees, which could lead them to focus on clinical oversight in these consulting efforts. Thus, it is critical that you take a structured approach to this year of consultation so that the focus remains on the golden opportunity to shape supervisory repertoires.

These requirements established by the BACB represent the minimum requirements for providing consulting support within the first year of certification. However, newly certified BCBAs will often need more than the bare minimum of consultation to succeed. They may also need guidance to succeed in their supervision of RBT supervisees as well as trainees (i.e., those pursuing fieldwork experience). Thus, it may be useful for those who are within their first year since certification to receive consultation on their supervision efforts regardless of whom they are supervising. According to the guidelines, a newly certified BCBA might never supervise someone who is pursuing fieldwork which would mean that they are not mandated to have a CS. However, providing great supervision using an organized curriculum is challenging the first time (at least) regardless of how long it has been since certification. Thus, we encourage the reader to consider offering a year of support to BCBAs on their initial supervisory efforts even if those efforts do not occur in the first year of certification. Those new BCBAs are likely supervising RBTs who are not trainees and would still benefit from support and mentoring on supervision.

The purpose of this workbook is to guide your efforts as a CS with the NSs whom you support. This workbook focuses on strategies to support the NS in managing tasks related to the supervision they provide. The accompanying *New Supervisor's Workbook* is a companion resource that the NS can use to enhance the effects of the consultation. These resources are designed to facilitate success whether the CS and NS are in the same organization or whether it is a separately contracted arrangement.

This guide provides 4 structured months and 8 months that can be individually designed for the BCBA's needs along with a month's worth of preparatory activities. In each month, we provide a pre-meeting reflection activity and deliverables for the NS to complete and a discussion guide for the CS to use during the subsequent meeting. A template for a meeting agenda is provided and all agendas include review of technical details (e.g., signing contracts, tracking hours and activities), as well as discussion of the deliverables. Suggestions for post-meeting tasks are provided so that the NS can implement follow-up actions throughout the month with their supervisees (e.g., RBTs, BCaBAs) and trainees pursuing fieldwork experience.

The topics for each month generally follow the content of LeBlanc, Sellers et al. (2020), including:

a. creating a positive, collaborative supervision relationship with trainees,
b. identifying pivotal professional skills (e.g., problem-solving, interpersonal and therapeutic relationship skills, learning-to-learn skills) that a trainee needs to develop or that the NS needs to more fully develop,
c. identifying and resolving problems in the supervisory relationship,
d. developing organizational and time management systems for supervision activities,
e. evaluating the effects of supervision,
f. and creating a curriculum and competencies to use in supervisory efforts.

In some months, the CS and NS can select the monthly consultation topic from a list based on the NS's recent self-assessment and needs identification. Although this pair of workbooks is intended to be used as a stand-alone resource to organize your efforts, it may also be useful to use the LeBlanc, Sellers et al (2020) text as an additional resource if you need more detailed information than is provided here.

In instances where the consulting relationship will not be intact for 12 full months, the CS can combine the content of certain chapters into one month or assign the NS to complete the final chapters independently using their guide and the resources provided in LeBlanc, Sellers et al. (2020). The CS who is supporting several NSs could also create a monthly group meeting for the NSs to provide additional support once the mandatory time frame for consultation has passed. Such a group could be opened up to individuals who are not required by the BACB to receive support (e.g., in their first year as a certificant but not yet supervising trainees, in their second year as a certificant without having supervised a trainee). However, remember that any group meetings will not meet the BACB requirement (i.e., these are extra supports rather than mandated ones).

As a CS, you can enhance the benefits of this year-long experience by engaging in your own series of self-reflection and assessment activities and logistics planning activities prior to beginning consultation. In the "Getting Ready" section, we provide tools to assist you with these efforts. You will evaluate your own skills and confidence as a supervisor. You will also explore your own learning history and examine the influences of your environment on your supervisory repertoires. You will explore your values related to supervising others, including NSs. You will decide where things related to your consulting efforts will be stored and accessed and you will gather resource materials for the NS. You will develop a document that describes the terms and expectations for your consulting relationship. If you are employed within the same organization, this document will likely be considered an agreement with a list of the CS's and NS's rights rather than a formal legal contract. If you and the NS are not employed in the same organization, you will definitely want an official legal contract document for your consulting services as you would have for any other consulting services.

Finally, we provide an agenda and resources for a pre-meeting to discuss the upcoming consultation, review the agreement/contract, and answer questions.

The material in this workbook may help you reflect on the strategies that you have been using and why you have used these strategies. It may give you additional perspective or new ideas and help you to share your wisdom, experience, and perspective with your junior colleagues. As a CS, you have an opportunity to shape the supervisory repertoires of new behavior analysts who will go on to supervise others in better and more meaningful ways because of your efforts. Both their current and future supervisees and clients will benefit from the support that you provide to the NS. The support you provide will create a powerful impact in their future supervisory efforts. In the profession of applied behavior analysis (ABA), BCBAs have many job responsibilities (e.g., managing a clinical caseload, conducting professional training, teaching courses, conducting research) in addition to supervising others. Some individuals may not feel prepared to provide supervision and, as a result, may not find supervision activities enjoyable. Your efforts during the next year are directly designed to prepare NSs to be capable and confident in their supervisory skills so that they find fulfillment and enjoyment in providing supervision.

You may find that you also benefit from the mentoring and consultation you provide. As you endeavor to put your goals, values, and strategies for effective supervision into words, you will likely grow professionally, become more flexible in your communication, and develop a deeper understanding of how and why you supervise the way you do (LeBlanc, Sellers et al., 2020). Perhaps you will experience renewed enthusiasm and passion for the discipline and satisfaction with this aspect of your professional life as you strengthen the skills of other supervisors. Your efforts represent a powerful way to do good in the world and to exponentially increase the positive impact you have on the profession (i.e., you mentor five people well who then each supervise five people and so on). We wish you well on this mentorship journey and we are honored to support your efforts with this workbook.

Getting Ready

The purpose of this section is to guide you through reflection on your skills and workload, your history, your values related to consulting to NSs as well as to get you organized on the logistics involved in embarking on this mentoring journey.

I. Self-Assessment and Self-Reflection

Self-Assessment

Skills and workload. Your analysis of your skills and workload will allow you to determine whether you have the capacity to support an NS and which professional and supervisory skill sets represent your strengths. For the relative weaknesses, this is your best opportunity to learn and grow along with the NS you are supporting. Use the Skills Assessment to self-evaluate important skill sets and use the resource table at the end of this chapter to shore up any areas needing development. The skills are divided into two categories: foundational skills and advanced supervision and mentoring skills. You will use all of these skills in your efforts with your NSs. Score each skill with one of the following codes: 1) developing, 2) proficient, 3) fluent. In addition, you can place an asterisk (*) by the score for any skill that you also think is problematic. The operational definitions for each score are provided on the assessment. The NSs you support will also be completing a version of this skills self-assessment and they will share the results with you. They will likely only have some of the foundational skills and only a few of the advanced skills as they are just starting to supervise others. As you work through the content for each month, many of those months will include additional, more detailed skills assessments for that particular topic.

Foundational Supervision Skills

Instructions: Rate each of the following supervision and mentorship skills as: 3) fluent, 2) proficient, 1) developing. Mark an asterisk (*) if your repertoire for this skill includes some problematic history and performance aspects (e.g., history of receiving harsh feedback and you sometimes behave the same way when you give feedback).

- Score 3 for *fluent* if you perform the skill accurately, consistently, quickly, and in the presence of distractors or adverse conditions.
- Score 2 for *proficient* if you perform the skill accurately and consistently with a little preparation, effort, and in the presence of only minimal distractors.
- Score 1 for *developing* if you are not yet able to perform the skill consistently and accurately, even under optimal conditions.

Specific Foundational Supervision Skill	Score
BACB Supervision Requirements	
1. Describe basic requirements (e.g., frequency of supervision, relevant activities, acceptable modalities, use of group supervision)	
2. Name, describe the purpose and how to use, and access required documents and forms	
3. Describe, create, use, and teach others how to use documentation systems	
4. Develop a contract and review the contract with a supervisee using an informed consent approach	
TOTAL:	/12
Purpose of Supervision	
1. Describe the purpose for implementing behavior-analytic supervision (e.g., the benefits and desired outcomes)	
2. Describe the potential risks of ineffective supervision (e.g., poor client outcomes, poor supervisee performance)	
TOTAL:	/6

Specific Foundational Supervision Skill	Score
Structuring Supervision	
1. Develop a positive rapport	
2. Schedule and run effective meetings based on LeBlanc & Nosik (2019) checklist	
3. Establish clear performance expectations for the trainee and supervisee	
4. Conduct assessments of the supervisee or trainee	
5. Select supervision goals based on an assessment to improve relevant skills (BACB Task List based and ethics)	
TOTAL:	/15
Training and Performance Management	
1. Explain the purpose of feedback and discuss preferences for trainee to receive and give feedback	
2. Use Behavior Skills Training (BST) in teaching supervisees and trainees	
3. Train personnel to competently perform assessment and intervention procedures	
4. Use performance monitoring, feedback, and reinforcement systems	
5. Use a functional assessment approach (e.g., performance diagnostics) and tools (Performance Diagnostic Checklist—Human Services; PDC-HS) to identify variables affecting personnel performance	
6. Use function-based strategies to improve personnel performance	
TOTAL:	/18
Evaluating the Effects of Supervision	
1. Solicit, review, and respond to feedback from supervises, trainees, and others	
2. Evaluate the effects of supervision (e.g., on client outcomes, on supervisee repertoires)	
3. Implement changes when needed	
TOTAL:	/9
Monitoring and Managing Stress and Wellness	
1. Monitor your own stress levels and detect the effects of stress on your supervisory skills and on others	
2. Engage in appropriate self-care strategies to manage stress (i.e., identify alternative behaviors when you notice you are impacted by stress)	
3. Teach supervisees and trainees to monitor their stress levels and detect effects on others	
4. Teach supervisees and trainees to engage in appropriate self-care strategies to manage stress	
TOTAL:	/12

Advanced Supervision and Mentoring Skills

Instructions: Rate each of the following supervision and mentorship skills as: 3) fluent, 2) proficient, 1) developing. Mark an asterisk (*) if your repertoire for this skill includes some problematic history and performance aspects (e.g., history of receiving harsh feedback and you sometimes behave the same way when you give feedback).

- Score 3 for *fluent* if you perform the skill accurately, consistently, quickly, and in the presence of distractors or adverse conditions.
- Score 2 for *proficient* if you perform the skill accurately and consistently with a little preparation, effort, and in the presence of only minimal distractors.
- Score 1 for *developing* if you are not yet able to perform the skill consistently and accurately, even under optimal conditions.

Specific Foundational Supervision Skill	Score
Maintaining Supervision	
1. Establish, and continually evaluate the health of bi-directional, collaborative supervisory relationships	
2. Self-monitor your reactions to various supervisees and mentees to detect potential fractures in the supervisory relationship	
3. Ask the supervisees open-ended questions to produce insight about their own actions, knowledge, and understanding	
4. Identify and address cultural variables in supervisory relationships	
5. Identify your own professional reinforcers to foster career sustainability	
6. Assist your supervisees and trainees to identify their professional reinforcers to foster career sustainability	
TOTAL:	/18

GETTING READY

Specific Foundational Supervision Skill	Score
Training and Performance Management	
1. Teach supervisees and trainees how to discuss and train feedback delivery and reception skills	
2. Prepare for and have crucial conversations with supervisees, families, colleagues, and supervisors	
3. Teach supervisees and trainees to prepare for and have crucial conversations with supervisees, families, colleagues, and supervisors	
4. Describe your own performance and the reasons why you performed that way while performing (i.e., a running, descriptive narrative while you are behaving)	
5. Teach supervisees and trainees how to self-observe and describe their performance and the reasons for it while performing (i.e., how to use a running narrative to describe why they do what they do)	
6. Teach supervisees and trainees to use Behavior Skills Training (BST)	
7. Guide supervisees and trainees through structured problem-solving analyses rather than solving problems for them	
8. Assess and address supervisees' and trainees' organization and time-management issues that impact professional performance	
9. Assess and address supervisees' and trainees' interpersonal-skill deficits that impact professional performance	
TOTAL:	/27
Evaluating the Effects of Supervision	
1. Teach supervisees and trainees to engage in self-evaluation	
2. Teach supervisees and trainees to solicit and evaluate feedback	
3. Teach supervisees and trainees to engage in self-monitoring	
TOTAL:	/9
Monitoring and Managing Stress and Wellness	
1. Create a structured self-monitoring plan to maintain self-care	
2. Access supports (e.g., colleagues, supervisors/mentors, professionals) to assist in problem-solving and managing stress	
3. Enhance and refine organization and time management (OTM) and problem-solving to decrease stress	
4. Teach supervisees and trainees to create a structured, self-monitoring plan to maintain self-care	
5. Teach supervisees and trainees to access supports (e.g., colleagues, supervisors/mentors, professionals) to assist in problem-solving and managing stress	
6. Teach supervisees and trainees to enhance and refine OTM and problem-solving to decrease stress	
TOTAL:	/18

Complete the workload analysis activity to determine whether your current duties and responsibilities will allow you to take on the task of mentoring NSs. For each task, consider all of your efforts in a month and fill in the total hours dedicated to that task. For example, if you have a full client caseload that requires approximately 30 hours a week of client-related activities, you might enter 120 (i.e., 30 X 4) in the time requirement for that category. You might have a lower direct caseload but more administrative and management duties (e.g., manage 4 BCBAs, manage the client intake team; 15 hours per week X 4 weeks = 60 hours). Some categories might not have any hours allocated (e.g., no service responsibilities to the profession).

If your NSs are using the corresponding workbook, the effort requirement for your consultation will be significantly lower but there will still be effort required to get ready, to plan for each month, and to meet with the NS. For consulting with an NS, count the hour of direct consultation and 1 additional hour of preparation per month. If you are consulting for more than one new BCBA, count 1 hour of preparation per 3 NSs. You should also guide the NS through completion of a similar workload analysis so that they can meet their ethical responsibilities to only take on the number of supervisees and trainees that they can actually support (BACB, 2020). They should repeat that analysis periodically throughout your consultation to ensure that they are not overcommitting and to shape their estimates of time allocation and capacity.

Monthly Workload Analysis

Task	Average Weekly Time Requirement	Facilitators	Barriers
Client Caseload Management			
RBT Caseload			
BCaBA Caseload			
Trainee Caseload			
Administrative Responsibilities			
Other Duties			
Total Average Weekly Work Hours			

Self-Reflection

History and Values. There are several potential advantages to reflecting on your history and the people who have had important and lasting impacts on your personal and professional lives (LeBlanc, Sellers et al., 2020). First, reflection allows us to be an active participant in our own learning, rather than simply having our behavior shaped by others. Reflection allows us to integrate past influences into our current professional activities by identifying important rules, lessons learned, and core values to guide our future decisions and our guidance for those we mentor. Your reflections will also help you to guide the NSs you mentor in their own reflections and identification of their values. The upcoming Mentor Tree activity will guide you through your self-reflection and values identification. Consider the following questions about those who appear on your tree:

- Who has served as a supervisor or mentor for you throughout your life? _____
_____

- What things did these supervisors do that you really liked? What things did they do that made you feel successful or supported? How did they create an environment of learning? _____
_____

    - What did you most value from each experience? _____
    _____

    - Can you see any of those behaviors in your own supervisory behavior? _____
    _____

- What things did these supervisors do that you did not like? What things did they do that made you feel unsuccessful or unsupported? What things did they do that presented barriers to your learning? _____
_____

    - Can you see any of those behaviors in your own supervisory behavior? _____
    _____

    - Have you ever expressly told a past supervisor what you liked about the supervisory experience with them? If not, consider calendaring some time to send a thank you email or note. _____
    _____

As you think about the various people who have influenced you, think about the conditions that were in effect for them while they were interacting with you. Were they new to their role (e.g., parent, supervisor, teacher) or experienced? Were they supported in their efforts, or does it seem as if they were operating under adverse circumstances? Considering these questions and the answers might reveal why a supervisor, mentor, or loved one behaved the way they did. Reflecting on the influences of those from our past and present affords the additional advantage of revealing ongoing professional development needs. For example, you might identify that you have never had experience with someone who fits the bill of a "great supervisor," yet you are trying to be one and to teach others how to be one. If this is the case, congratulations on recognizing this as a part of your history and taking action to try to be the supervisor you never had (Bailey & Burch, 2010). This workbook and the NS workbook will serve as important guides that may increase your confidence in your efforts and help you achieve your goals.

The Mentor Tree is divided into four parts that each represent a different part of the supervisor's learning journey: roots, trunk, branches, and acorns. The roots represent critical formative mentors who influenced your primary values, rules, and core repertoires early in life (e.g., parents, siblings, teachers, coaches). Some of these people may have inspired your later career pursuit or shaped the things you value (e.g., diversity and travel, volunteerism, education). The trunk represents those who influenced your basic professional repertoires (e.g., professors, practicum or fieldwork supervisors, peers). The branches represent continuing influences throughout your career who spark growth and learning and sponsor you for new opportunities. With career progress, peers begin to exert more influence and provide more support and modeling (e.g., a colleague who is unflappable during difficult conversations may give you tips and strategies for maintaining your composure). The acorns represent the next generation of future professionals that you have and will support as a supervisor, mentor, and consultant. Create your Mentor Tree specifying each formative influence and the impact that they have had on your personal or professional development and values.

This Mentor Tree will facilitate reflection on past and present influences of all types, including family, peers, teachers, supervisors, and mentors, among others. Begin with your roots (i.e., critical, formative influencers) and the impact each one had on your personal and professional development. Fill in the area around the roots by identifying people and their impact. Next, fill in the trunk using the names from the Chapter 1 activity where you identified your prior supervisors. For each name, try to specify the influence this person had on you, the lessons you learned, and the specific behaviors you want to imitate or that you want to avoid imitating. As you summarize the central influences, reflect on each person's likely motivations, individual and cultural learning histories, and the person's specific actions you hope to emulate. For the branches, decide whether to take a retrospective, prospective or both approaches to further growth. Identify the influences of many life and career influencers that are not represented elsewhere on your tree and consider where you wsnt to focus your next career steps and the people you might want to recruit as mentors. In the section of mentees, the acorns represent the oppoertunity to influence others who are just beginning in their careers. List some of the core values you want to influence in your supervisees and mentees.

Life and career mentors

_____
_____
_____

Basic foundation mentors

_____
_____
_____

Mentees

_____
_____
_____

Critical formative mentors

_____
_____
_____

Reprinted with permission from Sloan Publishing

After filling in your Mentor Tree, complete the Values Identification Activity to explore your professional values related to practice (i.e., the work you do with clients and families to create and deliver their programming) and supervising and mentoring others (i.e., the work you do with other professionals to strengthen their repertoires). Values are not the same as goals. While goals can be achieved, values are aspirational guides towards which we continually work (Chase et al., 2013). What are the top 2-3 things you value about providing supervision? Maybe it's consumer protection, establishing a passion for life-long learning in others, or the health and success of the profession. Identifying and responding toward your core values for supervision can help you make decisions and sustain your supervisory practices even when things are difficult.

Think about the individuals listed in the acorn section, how you want to influence them, and some of the strategies that you intend to use to build a strong collaborative bidirectional relationship with them. Describe your aspirational goals for yourself as a supervisor and the strategies that you want to use during supervision. You might refer to LeBlanc, Sellers et al. (2020) Chapter 3 for additional support and guidance in these self-reflection activities. As an example of a value related to practice, Linda LeBlanc identifies behaving compassionately as a value. An example of behaving consistently with this value is actively listening to a family's goals for services and involving the family in collaborative decision making about treatment. To convey this value to NSs, she uses perspective taking exercises to help an NS imagine what it might be like for families of children with autism. For a supervision related value, healthy relationships with supervisees are important to her. She tries to behave consistently with this value by getting to know each person that she supervisees and supports. One strategy that she has used to help establish that value for an NS is introducing them to the Collaboration Activity in LeBlanc, Sellers et al. (2020) and describing how they might use it with their supervisees and trainees.

Values Identification Activity

Domain	Value	Example of Behaving Consistently with this Value	Strategy for Conveying this Value or Helping to Establish it for NS
Practice			
Supervision			

II. Logistics and Agreement/Contract Preparation

Logistics. You and the NS you support will need a well-organized and efficient means to collaborate, share information, and document your efforts. Logistics management represents a great opportunity for you to model being organized, planful and responsible for your consultation efforts. Convey to your NS why you plan so carefully and why it is critically important that they do the same thing with their supervisees and trainees.

- Identify your available and preferred electronic file share options (e.g., Dropbox, Box, Sharefile) that can be accessed post-termination of the consultation for audit purposes
- Identify your file naming structure for monthly documentation
- Gather and store any materials that you will give the NS (e.g., articles, meeting agenda templates)
- Identify who will create the calendar invitation for meetings
- Identify the meeting platform that will be used if the meetings are conducted remotely
- Identify an optimal recurring meeting time in the first week of the month. You will confer with the NS on overlapping availability in your pre-meeting (described below)

Contract Development. As with any other professional relationship, you will need a contract that specifies each person's roles, responsibilities, rights, and limitations. The NS needs the support of their CS and is mandated to document that ongoing support. There are important rights and protections to consider for the NS who is in a position of dependence upon the CS. In addition, the CS needs clear documentation of the conditions that are required for continuation of the consultation relationship and documentation of support.

If both parties are employed by the same organization, there may or may not be any compensation for the consulting services beyond the compensation already available as salary. If the CS and NS are not employed at the same organization, there may be compensation for the CS for the services that are being provided to the NS. Each party must fully understand and commit to the conditions of the relationship. In addition to specifying the conditions of the consulting relationship, the approach used in establishing and discussing the relationship provides an excellent model for the NS to imitate in their efforts with their new supervisees and trainees. Use the considerations below to guide your efforts in creating a consulting contract for your services. These considerations are offered only as general information as a starting point for you and should not be taken as legal advice. When drafting your contract, it is critical to access support from a professional who is familiar with local and state laws and requirements.

Considerations for Developing a Supervision Contract

- Specify the scope and content of the consultation (i.e., on supervision activities rather than basic practice of behavior analysis, does not constitute responsibility or liability for the supervisee's actions)
- Specify the duration of the contract and what should happen if the contract needs to be amended
- Specify any compensation provided for the services
- Specify the expectations for both the CS and NS
- Describe the conditions under which the contract will terminate (e.g., a specific date, upon mutual agreement by either party, violations of the law or BACB ethics requirements that pose a risk of harm to others, following X number of failed attempts to remediate a performance problem)
- Require that both parties agree to uphold the BACB Code of Ethics for Behavior Analysts and RBT Ethics Code (2.0)
- Describe the steps to be taken if there is a disagreement between the parties
- Attest that both parties meet all requirements to enter into the contract

Pre-Meeting. As with any professional relationship, it is important to carefully establish the relationship with a strong foundation by creating clear expectations for both parties and collaborating to determine your path forward. Your pre-meeting will help you do this. Before having your first month's consultation, schedule a meeting to review your contract or agreement for consultation and your plan for the year. This will be easier if both you and the NS are simultaneously using these workbooks, as they are designed to be parallel tools to help you structure your interactions.

Since your consultation time with the NS will likely be limited to one hour per month, it is important that each of you plan carefully to maximize the use of your shared meeting time. Follow recommended strategies for planning and conducting effective meetings as described by LeBlanc and Nosik (2019). Leach et al., (2009) identified 5 design characteristics that impact the perceived quality of a meeting:

1. use of an agenda,
2. notetaking,
3. punctuality,
4. having an appropriate environment, and
5. having a meeting leader.

Use an agenda to plan and manage your meeting so that both you and the NS can prepare for the meeting. Agendas should include the purpose of the meeting, each task, and a time estimate for completion of each task (LeBlanc & Nosik, 2019). As the CS, you should create the meeting agenda for the pre-meeting and the first few months, but the NS should be developing the subsequent meetings for the consultation each month. If you and the NS already know each other and have worked together for a while, you can probably conduct the pre-meeting in 30 minutes. If you are consulting with an NS that you do not know well, you should have a 60-minute pre-meeting.

Sharing information with participants in advance of a meeting can substantially improve the effectiveness of the meeting by clarifying expectations and prompting preparation (LeBlanc & Nosik, 2019). Bailey and Burch (2010) recommend sharing an agenda at least 24 hours in advance of the meeting and Fienup et al (2013) suggest using email reminders about the upcoming meeting. Here is a suggested agenda to structure your pre-meeting and plan to distribute your agenda at least 24 hours in advance of your pre-meeting.

Pre-Meeting Agenda

Attendees, Time, Date, and Location

1. Introductions and background/values share (if appropriate, delete if not necessary): (15 min.)
    a. Convey values and approach to practice and supervision from the values identification activity.
2. Review of expectations and contract (if appropriate, shorten if no contract required): (15 min.)
3. Discuss logistics of monthly consultation: (15 min.)
    a. Use of workbooks
    b. Review of resources (e.g., articles, meeting agenda templates)
    c. Preferred communication modality
    d. Preferred electronic file share options (e.g., Dropbox, Box, Sharefile) and file naming structure for monthly documentation
    e. Identify who will create the calendar invitation for meetings and the preferred meeting platform or locations
    f. Identify the recurring meeting time in the first week of the month
4. Meeting wrap up: (1-5 min.)

If you need to have a formal contract, bring the contract to the meeting and review it, answer questions, sign it, and make sure each party leaves with a copy of the signed contract or shared access to an electronic copy. Discuss the logistics for ongoing meetings relying on the checklist that you used to prepare for this discussion (see prior section). Discuss your communication preferences and shared storage options. Identify a recurring meeting time that occurs in the first week of the month if possible.

Planning the Course of Consultation. Some of the NSs with whom you consult may be beyond the 1-year window where a full year is required. Some may have already mastered basic skills and need additional focus on more advanced skills. We provide two examples of how to link a self-assessment to your planning with each NS after your pre-meeting, first month, and review of their self-assessment. The Specific Skills sections in this workbook can be used as resources for months 4-11 with the selection of skills based on their assessment. In these examples you will note that these two NSs start their consultation with the CS in different months (e.g., Feb 2021, June 2021). However, Month 1 will always refer to the first month of activities after the Pre-Meeting associated with Getting Ready. In addition, Appendix A at the end of the workbook provides a planning guide that has entries for multiple NSs that could be used over the span of a few years of consulting.

The first case example is J.P. who is a brand newly certified BCBA who needs to take on a trainee within one month of passing the exam. J.P. is eager to learn, hard-working, used to studying and reading, and needs to learn everything from top to bottom as they have not yet supervised any RBTs or anyone else for that matter. J.P. has done BST before in the role of trainer for new RBTs. The first three months include starting strong with respect to logistics, relationships, expectations, collaboration and reciprocal feedback; assessing skills and identifying teaching priorities for a curricular roadmap. After a review of their initial self-assessment, the CS decides that it is important to start with the basics of providing high quality training using BST and feedback and conducting basic performance monitoring. This skill set will be important for efforts with RBTs as well as trainees and it is important that J.P. can already do what they will need to teach their trainee to do (e.g., conduct integrity checks, provide acceptable and positive feedback). The plan moves on to work on skills that enhance learning, such as being able to describe why you do what you do (i.e., a narrative of your actions and choices) for a trainee or supervisee and how to debrief after certain types of observations (e.g., delayed feedback and debrief after you have observed someone else giving feedback). Next, the plan incorporates how to evaluate the effects of your supervision. For example, if J.P. is now collecting integrity data and providing feedback, there should be at least one source of information about the effects of that feedback on procedural integrity. The next month involves reassessment of skills. It turns out J.P. has made wonderful progress and improvements in almost every foundational skill. It is time to begin focusing on more advanced skills such as using a structured problem-solving approach and organization and time management skills for both J.P. and any of J.P.'s future trainees. The eleventh month focuses on assessing scope of competence. This final month focuses on goal setting for continued learning and greater engagement with the community of practice that has been built over the year.

Let's contrast this example with T.A. who has been a BCBA for 3 years, but has not yet supervised a trainee. T.A. has supervised many RBTs and is fluent at collecting procedural integrity data, providing feedback, and using BST to establish new skills for these RBTs. However, the majority of these experiences training and supervising others have focused on entry level treatment and data collection skills and T.A. feels uncertain about what to teach and how to teach a person who is trying to learn the skills necessary to be a BCBA. After the first three months (i.e., these should always be the first three months), the plan jumps ahead beyond feedback and performance monitoring to feedback and difficult conversations, skills for enhancing learning, therapeutic relationships, self-care, and public presentations. These topics have been chosen because they feel like areas where T.A. wants more support to develop competence and confidence in both use of these skills and in supporting others in using them. This curricular plan also finishes with assessing scope of competence and transition out of consulting services.

Sample Completed Yearly Planning Guide/Roadmap for New Supervisor

BCBA Initials:____	Example 1: J.P. Brand new BCBA who needs it all	Example 2: T.A. BCBA with 3 yrs experience but no trainees
Month 1	Planning Logistics and Building Relationships: Feb 2021	Planning Logistics and Building Relationships: June 2021
Month 2	Assessing and Self-Assessing: Mar 2021	Assessing and Self-Assessing: April 2021
Month 3	Curricular Roadmap and Competencies: April 2021	Curricular Roadmap and Competencies: August 2021
Month 4	Teaching Effectively Using BST	Feedback and Difficult Conversations
Month 5	Ongoing Monitoring and Performance Management	Evaluating the Effects of Supervision
Month 6	Feedback and Difficult Conversations	Enhancing Learning
Month 7	Enhancing Learning	Problem-solving and Decision Making
Month 8	Problem-solving and Decision Making	Compassionate Care and Therapeutic Relationships
Month 9	Evaluating the Effects of Supervision	Self-Care
Month 10	Organization and Time Management	Public Speaking and Professional Presentations
Month 11	Scope of Competence	Scope of Competence
Month 12	Professional Development Planning	Professional Development Planning

Thank you for the time and effort that you are investing to prepare for your upcoming efforts with the NS who needs your support and guidance! Well Done! Take a breath and give yourself some well-deserved praise for taking a structured approach to your consultation services. Your efforts will benefit that NS and ALL of their supervisees and trainees. The time you spend with this NS may be some of the most impactful experiences of their career and it may well help you evolve your own supervisory style and practices. You can use the checklist below to make sure that you did not miss any tasks from the Getting Ready section.

Getting Ready Checklist

- ☐ Complete Skills Assessment

- ☐ Complete Workload Analysis

- ☐ Complete Mentor Tree

- ☐ Complete Values Identification Activity

- ☐ Complete Logistics Planning

    - ☐ Identify your available and preferred electronic file share options (e.g., Dropbox, Box, Sharefile)

    - ☐ Identify your file naming structure for monthly documentation

    - ☐ Gather and store any materials that you will give the NS (e.g., articles, meeting agenda templates)

    - ☐ Identify who will create the calendar invitation for meetings

    - ☐ Identify the meeting platform that will be used if the meetings are conducted remotely

    - ☐ Identify an optimal recurring meeting time in the first week of the month. You will confer with the NS on overlapping availability in your pre-meeting (described below)

- ☐ Complete Contract Preparation

- ☐ Arrange a Time for the Pre-Meeting

- ☐ Create and Distribute Your Pre-Meeting Agenda to the NS

Month to Month Guides:
The Early Months

The remaining chapters structure your monthly activities with your NS. For each month there is an outline of important information that you should convey to the NS to guide their actions. We provide detailed outlines, but you will want to add in your own wisdom and examples for each topic. The first few months are pre-set because the topics of those months are important for anyone who is beginning to supervise. They focus on building strong relationships, managing logistics and stress, assessing your own needs and those of your trainee, and planning your curriculum based on those needs.

As a CS you only have one required meeting per month with the NS. However, the NS will have more than one meeting with their trainee. You will need to double check each month that their supervision activities with their trainees meet the BACB requirements regarding the number of contacts and direct observations with clients per month. As the CS you can help the NS identify which activities are best carried out in their trainee meeting(s) and observation(s) in a given month.

The topics to be addressed in months 4 through 11 will be selected by you and the NS using the information from their self-reflection and self-assessment activities. We can't tell you which specific skills they will need and when, but the examples provided in Getting Ready should help you recommend an order. The first half of the year will likely focus on honing the NS's basic supervision skills, whereas the second half generally will focus on developing more advanced skills. Planning is important, but keep in mind that you need to be flexible. You and the NS will use data from their self-assessments and your joint evaluation of the effects of your consulting sessions to revisit topics, reorder topics, or add in new topics. You and the NS can choose to spend an additional month on a topic or move forward to a topic that has suddenly become pressing or relevant (e.g., crucial conversations topic was scheduled for month 8, but in month 5 they realize they need to have one with their trainee now).

Each month the NS will be engaging in preparation activities for the meeting with you and for their supervision activities with their trainees. Each of those activities focuses on tasks to enhance their skills as a supervisor and they will benefit from reviewing those activities with you. They will then use information from that preparation and your consultation to inform their supervision activities throughout the remainder of the month. This workbook and the NS workbook are designed to create a first year of supervising that is dynamic and multifaceted. Picture an infinity symbol with you, as the CS on the right. The NS is in the center and their supervisees are on the right. The loop on the left represents your interactions with the NS and the loop on the right represents the NS's interactions with their trainees and supervisees. The NS is engaging in self-reflection, assessment, and planning activities to grow their skill set and discussing the results of those activities with you. They are then guiding and assisting their trainees in doing similar self-reflections, self-assessments, and goal planning. Finally, all your efforts flow back around to you through the NS as they evaluate their practices and their effects and review them with you for continual improvement. You are having a direct effect on the NS and an indirect effect on their trainees.

Creating this infinite flow of information is a tall order, but one that we think you will find enjoyable and transformative. In your efforts with the NS, you will need to impact their knowledge and skills as a supervisor, and you will need to impact their ability to increase the knowledge and skills of their trainees as well. You should also focus on increasing their pivotal professional repertoires (e.g., interpersonal communication, organization and time management, problem-solving) so that they become well prepared to succeed independently as a supervisor. At this point you are well positioned to start your consulting relationship off on the right foot! You have engaged in thoughtful reflection, assessment, and planning and you are ready to get started with Month 1!

Month 1
Planning Logistics and Building Relationships

Goals for Upcoming Meeting

- Maintain and strengthen your collaborative relationship with the NS.
- Convey the value of using agendas and model using an agenda for supervision.
- Review Workload Assessment.
- Review tasks and scripts for their first meeting with trainees.
- Answer any questions they have about the first month of supervision.

The NS should have been diligently preparing for their meeting with you. Their workbook prompts them to engage in several tasks that will allow the two of you to make the most of your limited time together. Here is a list of what they have been working on:

- Reviewing the tasks from the Getting Ready section and organizing their documents (e.g., contracts, tracking forms) for their first month of meetings with you and with their trainees.
- Completing and sending you their self-assessment and draft goals for review.
- Completing a values identification activity similar to the one that you completed and shared in the Getting Ready meeting.
- Preparing their script for how to explain the value of feedback and why it is important that it is bi-directional.

These items will make up much of the content of your meeting with them. However, there is one additional item for the meeting agenda—using agendas to prepare for effective meeting. You will be the one preparing this content and this chapter is designed to help you do that. You will be providing the agenda for the Month 1 meeting, and you will serve as the meeting leader. We have provided that agenda for you and we have included the critical components of an effective agenda:

1. all items covered in the meeting,
2. the items arranged in a logical progression,
3. a time estimate for each item,
4. the total of the estimates does not exceed the time available, and
5. a wrap up and planning for next actions and the next meeting.

The italicized items are for your information to guide your actions while the numbered items constitute the actual agenda that you share with the other meeting attendee.

Agenda for Month 1 – CS version

1. Welcome (5 min.)
    a. How do you feel about the Getting Ready meeting and activities?
    b. Are you feeling ready for this meeting and the upcoming month?
2. Review of NSWorkload Assessment (3-5 min.)
    a. Evaluate any risks with taking on trainee(s)
    b. Provide ideas to mitigate risk if needed
3. Value of Agendas and how to prepare them (20 min.)
    a. Establish value of being organized and planning ahead to make the most of shared time
    b. Review the core features of an agenda
    c. Demonstrate how to use these ideas for planning observation of trainee and assess their understanding
4. Review of trainee logistics and contract for upcoming meetings (5 min.)
    a. Do they have access to everything and is it organized? If not, provide feedback and ideas for improvement
5. Review of NS Values Identification Activity (5 min.)
    a. Briefly remind them of the values example you shared last week
    b. Tell me a little bit more about one of your values and what led you to identify that as important to you
6. Review feedback questions and starter script for use with trainees (10 min.)
    a. You will be establishing your relationship with this new trainee and establishing the value of feedback in your relationship. How will you do that?
    b. Let's practice what you will say
    c. Provide feedback on their facial expression, body language, and content of their script to help them improve the content and delivery
    d. If their script and delivery are great, do a role-play where you are the new trainee and you give them options to respond to: 1) very hesitant trainee, 2) totally at ease trainee who is ready for feedback, 3) overly assertive trainee who indicates that they probably won't need any feedback
7. Review of use of Collaboration Activity (3-5 min.)
8. Wrap up (3-5 min.)
    a. Review action items for each party
    b. Set the next meeting time and date

Agenda to Share with NS 24 hours in advance

1. Welcome (5 min.)
2. Review of NS Workload Assessment (3-5 min.)
3. Value of Agendas and how to prepare them (20 min.)
4. Review of trainee logistics and contract for upcoming meetings (5 min.)
5. Review of NS values identification activity (5 min.)
6. Review feedback questions and starter script for use with trainees (10 min.)
7. Review of use of Collaboration Activity (3-5 min.)
8. Wrap up (3-5 min.)

Welcome

This item comes first on the agenda because it logically needs to. However, opening with questions about their experience reaffirms your commitment to a collaborative, bi-directional relationship. This helps you meet your first goal—to maintain and strengthen the relationship. Your version of the agenda provides a few open ended (i.e., non-yes/no) questions to get you started but feel free to substitute or add questions to this item. However, make sure that you do not go over the allotted time because you are also modeling how to conduct a meeting effectively, which includes remaining on track with your agenda. The one exception would be if the NS is indicating that they feel overwhelmed and is responding with strong emotions. In that case, you would spend a little extra time calming them and reassuring them that the preparation that they are engaging in will help them be successful as an NS. Remember, they are looking to you as a model of how to establish strong, trusting relationships with supervisees, so plan your approach to this item to provide a good example of how to get started in a meeting with a new supervisee or trainee.

Review of NS Workload Assessment

Review the results of their workload assessment with them. This item comes second on the agenda because it is important to determine whether this NS actually has the capacity to take on trainees before they move any farther in the process. Explain to the NS that there are risks in taking on this responsibility without the capacity to do it well. If the NS responded to the welcome questions with demonstrations of anxiety and stress, your analysis of their workload may help you identify why this occurred (i.e., they are already overcommitted). If there are no concerns or minor concerns, indicate your support and that you will have them repeat this activity periodically because circumstances can change. They will be prompted to repeat the analysis every few months in their NS workbook.

👥 Value of Agendas and How to Prepare Them

LeBlanc and Nosik (2019) provide guidance on planning and leading effective meetings. You might assign this article to the NS as a resource for their professional development in general and for more detailed guidance on structuring and leading supervision meetings. Your goal with this agenda item is to establish the value of being organized and planning ahead to make the most of shared time. You are also modeling being organized and planning ahead in creating a distributing your agenda for this meeting 24 hours in advance. The NS has several items to prepare, and you are setting the expectation that they are ready to cover each of those things in this meeting. It is important for the NS to master this skill quickly if they have not already done so. It is also important for the trainee to start developing these skills slowly throughout their fieldwork under the guidance of the NS. Use the following information to prepare your coverage of meetings and agendas.

Leach et al. (2009) identified 5 design characteristics that impact the perception of a meeting as "good":

1. use of an agenda,
2. keeping of minutes,
3. punctuality (i.e., start on time, end on time),
4. appropriate meeting environment, and
5. having a meeting leader.

Although you will be addressing the use of agendas and meeting management in the context of supervision meetings, the same principles apply to many of the meetings in which behavior analysts are engaged (e.g., supervision, treatment implementation, parent collaboration and training, case coordination, behavior program training, individual education plan development, class, research). In fact, one could argue that the "difference between an ineffective meeting an a productive, and fun meeting is in the behavior of those planning and leading the meetings." (LeBlanc & Nosik, 2019, p. 697)

The agenda is a planning tool that facilitates preparation before the meeting and time management during the meeting. The agenda should include each task or topic to be covered in the meeting, and a time estimate for coverage of each item. The total time allocated to the items should not exceed the time that is available for the meeting. In fact, there should be slightly less time allocated on the agenda than time in the meeting. For example, a 30 minute meeting should only have 25 allocated minutes for content to allow time to arrive and transition out of the meeting.

The meeting leader often develops the preliminary agenda and then seeks input on the agenda from the other parties. Many of the items on a supervision agenda should be standing items (e.g., review of documentation, client data review, client questions and concerns, competency test) after the first few meetings. Once the items are generated for the agenda, the meeting organizer should arrange them in an order that follows logically and provide an estimated duration for each. The order of the agenda items should follow the likely flow of discussion and the priority of the items.

You can also monitor how long each item actually takes in order to refine your ability to estimate the time and effort associated with tasks.

Sellers et al. (2016) recommends teaching supervisees and trainees how to develop and submit a supervision meeting agenda at least 24 hours in advance of each meeting. This process may occur throughout the course of the supervisory relationship and the earlier this topic is reviewed, the better. The task of creating or contributing to an agenda requires the trainee to reflect on the items that are relevant to their training goals, which in turn meets the goals of having a collaborative, bi-directional supervisory relationship. The supervisor then provides feedback on the agenda (e.g., re-order the items according to priority, eliminate or add items).

As the CS, you will prepare and distribute the agenda for Month 1, Month 2, and Month 3. In Month 4 you will begin to transition this responsibility to the NS. Providing the agenda for the first few months allows them to see multiple exemplars of your agenda preparation and management before having to do this task themselves later in your relationship. However, the NS will either be preparing and distributing agendas for their meetings with their trainees or editing their trainee's agendas throughout all months of supervised fieldwork. Consider having them show you their agendas for those meetings and provide feedback. Also consider having them report on their self-monitoring efforts in terms of the extent to which their supervision meetings go according to plan (e.g., their time estimates are correct, the order of the topics was appropriate).

Review of Logistics and Contract for Trainee

The NS workbook provides several prompts and instructions to guide the NS through making sure that they have all the documents that they will need for use with their trainees ready to go. Templates and samples are provided in their workbook for several of the documents as indicated below. These documents should be ready to go, and the NS may or may not have questions for you about some of these topics:

- the initial agenda for the trainee supervision meetings (template provided)
- the agenda for observations (sample provided)
- the trainee contract
- tracking documents for hours, topics, and feedback
- a plan for managing shared documents and carrying out reviews/edits
- ideas for group supervision

Review of NS Values Identification Activity

You completed a values identification activity and talked about your values in the pre-meeting with the NS. Now, the NS will have encountered the same activity in their workbook. You have modeled one potential response and now they should have prepared some responses of their own. This activity and the subsequent discussion with you are designed to prepare them to talk to their trainees about their professional values related to practice and supervising others. Ask the NS to describe their values for supervision as they would to their trainee in the initial meeting as a way of building rapport. It's okay if the NS is not fluent yet or sounds nervous as they practice with you – this is likely the first time have encountered such an activity. If you detect that they are anxious, let them know that is a totally reasonable response. As a reminder, here is the table that guided you and the NS through this activity.

Domain	Value	Example of Behaving Consistently with this Value	Strategy for Conveying this Value to Your Trainee
Practice			
Supervision			

Review Feedback Questions and Starter Script

One of the keys to a successful supervisory relationship is establishing effective bi-directional feedback from day one. This means that the NS needs to be prepared to talk about feedback and bi-directionality in the very first meeting with their trainee. They have encountered sample scripts in their workbook. These sample script are re-printed here for your convenience. They have also been referred to LeBlanc, Sellers et al. (2020) for more sample scripts. They should have reflected on their history with feedback and how they will share their experiences and convey their commitment to giving AND receiving feedback. They have also encountered several topic prompts to guide preparation of a script for how they will talk with their trainees about feedback in the first meeting before introducing the collaboration activity to them. The topic prompts that they encountered are printed below. Ask them to share their responses and to practice their script with you as a role-play. Provide feedback on the content and their delivery (e.g., body language, tone, facial expressions, speed) to help them get ready for their first meeting with their trainee. If their script and delivery are great from the first example, do a role-play where you are the new trainee and you give them options to respond to you as:

1. a very hesitant trainee,
2. totally at ease trainee who is ready for feedback, and/or
3. an overly assertive trainee who indicates that they probably won't need any feedback.

Sample Feedback Starter Scripts

- I'd love to hear about your past experiences with receiving feedback. What types of "feedback givers" have you experienced in the past?

- When I say "bi-directional feedback" I mean that feedback flows both ways between us and that it impacts both of us.

- Feedback is really important because it is one of the most direct and immediate ways that we can impact each other's behavior.

- I am committed to your success, which means I will be providing a lot of feedback to you. I am going to do my best to create a trusting relationship so that you can also help me improve by telling me what is working well and what might need some tweaking.

Draft Scripts

Questions to learn about trainee's history with feedback: _____
_____
_____
_____

Describing bi-directional feedback: _____
_____
_____
_____

Describing why feedback is critical: _____
_____
_____
_____

Describing how you and trainee will implement bi-directional feedback: _____
_____
_____
_____

 Trainee Collaboration Activity

The NS has encountered the Collaboration Activity as a tool that they can use to facilitate rapport building with their trainee in Month 1. They need to introduce this activity at the end of the first meeting, assign it as a follow up task, and then review it a subsequent meeting in Month 1. They should have reviewed the activity in preparation for this meeting, but you should be prepared to answer any questions about the activity and how to introduce it to their trainees. The purpose of this activity is to set the stage for a strong collaborative relationship between supervisor and trainee. This activity focuses on giving the trainee a structured opportunity to think about and discuss topics like receiving and giving feedback and goals that they may have for themselves. Having trainees complete this activity and then reviewing it with them increases the likelihood that the trainee will feel comfortable discussing these topics, as they will come into the conversation having had the opportunity to reflect on and develop their answers. This can be helpful for individuals who may feel put on the spot when asked these types of questions and struggle coming up with a meaningful response in the moment. During the first month of supervision, the NS will give a copy of this activity to their trainee in the first meeting and review it in the second meeting. The NS should be able to describe the activity and its purpose. Ask the NS whether they have any questions about the activity and what their plan is for presenting the activity to their trainee. The Collaboration Activity has been provided at the end of this chapter for your convenience.

Wrap Up

You are providing a model of a well-run meeting. This means that you want to make sure that you start your wrap up with sufficient time left in the meeting (i.e., at least 5-8 mins remaining). It is never appropriate to eliminate this item from the agenda because you have fallen behind on other items. It would be OK to defer questions about the collaboration activity to a follow up email, but you should not end the meeting without setting the time for the next meeting, make a list of follow up action items, and leaving time for each person to transition to their next meeting.

Reflection and Goal Evaluation

After you have completed the Month 1 consultation, reflect on the goals for this month and evaluate how well your efforts met those goals.

- Maintain and strengthen your collaborative relationship with the NS
- Convey the value of using agendas and model using an agenda for supervision
- Review NS Workload Assessment
- Review tasks and scripts for their first meeting with trainees
- Answer any questions they have about the first month of supervision

You may want to send a follow up email thanking the NS for their participation in the meeting and checking up on any items from the agenda that were not completed or any goals that were not met. Make any notes from your reflections here and use these notes to help you prepare for Month 2:

_____
_____
_____
_____

Preparation Checklist for Next Month:

- [ ] Review Materials from the NS
    - [ ] Self-Assessment results
    - [ ] Draft-Goals

- [ ] Complete the Assessment of Culturally Responsive and Humble Practices provided in the next month to enhance your discussion of culture with the NS

 Collaboration Activity for Trainees

Trainee Name: _____   Due Date: _____

The purpose of this activity is to set the stage for a strong, collaborative relationship between supervisor and trainee. This activity focuses on providing you with a structured opportunity to think about and discuss topics like receiving and giving feedback and goals that you may have for yourself. You'll review this activity in a meeting with your supervisor but taking the time to think about and answer the questions should help to make the conversation more comfortable. Talking about feedback can be new to some people and can make people feel nervous. The hope is that being able to complete this on your own time will minimize you feeling put on the spot when talking about feedback and will facilitate a meaningful conversation about feedback that will help you and your supervisor start out strong. Once you are done completing this form, email or save it to a shared drive 48 hours before the meeting in which you will review it with your supervisor.

1. What are at least three things you think you are good at and are excited to show me:

   _____
   _____
   _____

2. What are at least three things you are excited to learn about during your supervised fieldwork experience?

   _____
   _____
   _____

3. What professional skills are you most excited to learn about from me during supervision? (Check all that apply)

   ☐ organization   ☐ writing   ☐ difficult conversations

   ☐ time management   ☐ presenting   ☐ other: _____

   ☐ problem-solving   ☐ effective communication _____

4. When you think of "feedback," what specifically, does that mean to you and how do you feel? Why? What experiences contributed to your thoughts and feelings?

   _____
   _____
   _____

5. How do you prefer to receive praise? (Check all that apply)

   ☐ in the moment ☐ privately ☐ vocally (tell me)

   ☐ after the performance ☐ in writing ☐ I need help to figure this out

6. How do you prefer to receive corrective feedback?

   ☐ in the moment ☐ privately ☐ vocally (tell me)

   ☐ after the performance ☐ in writing ☐ I need help to figure this out

7. How comfortable are you giving me (your supervisor) direct feedback?

   ☐ pretty comfortable ☐ nervous, but I think I can do it ☐ scared & hesitant

   ☐ are you kidding me? I don't even know how to answer this.

8. How do you think you would prefer to give me (your supervisor) feedback about how our supervision is going?

   ☐ Let's have a standing agenda item so we can discuss in our meetings.

   ☐ I'll send you my feedback in an email after our meetings.

   ☐ I'll just bring things up in meetings as they come up.

   ☐ I am nervous about giving you feedback and think I am going to need help with how and when to do this.

Month 2
Assessing and Self-Assessing

Goals for Upcoming Meeting

- Maintain and strengthen your relationship with the NS.
- Review the first month of supervision with trainees.
- Review trainee documentation to ensure accuracy.
- Discuss the results of the NS self-assessment implications for months 4-6.
- Discuss the plan for self-assessment and assessment with trainees.
- Discuss core features of culturally responsive and humble supervisory and clinical practices and the results of your self-assessment.
- Identify any potential cultural differences that could impact your relationship with the new supervisor.

The NS has now been providing fieldwork supervision for a month and may have had 2-3 contacts with their trainee as well as several contacts with other RBT supervisees. This should have given them ample opportunity to create agendas for their contacts, explain the value of supervision, explain and discuss the results of the collaboration activity, sign a contract for supervision, and begin working on documentation of hours accrual with their trainee. They have also been diligently preparing for their Month 2 meeting with you. Their workbook prompts them to engage in several tasks that will allow the two of you to make the most of your limited time together. Here is a list of what they have already sent you and what they have been preparing:

1. Their self-assessment was sent to you in the Getting Ready month. You should have carefully reviewed these results and considered whether you have any other data that would confirm or disconfirm the accuracy of the self-assessment. You should also review the list of topics for which we have provided available resources so that you can choose the content of your meetings for months 4, 5, and 6.

2. The draft goals for this year were also sent to you. Review those carefully and consider those goals as you select the topics for your individualized focus.

3. Reflection Activity for Month 1 of supervision: The NS completed this activity to prepare for the Month 2 meeting with you. They should be in a great position to give you a concise update on what has occurred in their supervision sessions, highlighting any specific points of celebration or concern. They should also have trainee documentation to show you so that you can identify any errors.

4. Plan for trainee self-assessment and assessment activities: The NS should have the beginnings of a plan for assessing their trainee's skills and having the trainee self-assess as well. It may need more details or alterations in timing for certain assessments, so be prepared to offer them feedback and suggestions in a positive, supportive manner. You may need to guide them to simplify their plan or to be more specific with their language or criteria.

These items will make up much of the content of your meeting with them. However, there is one additional item for the meeting agenda – the importance of cultural responsiveness in supervision and clinical practices. You will be the one preparing this content and this chapter is designed to help you do that. You will talk about the results of your own self-assessment and assign them to complete it for themselves the following month. You will serve as the meeting leader for your consultation meeting for the upcoming Month 2 meeting, as well as next month (i.e., Month 3). Beginning with the Month 4 meeting you will turn over the agenda preparation to the NS, unless you have detected any performance issues related to creating effective agendas and running meetings. We have provided the agenda for you, and we have included a summary of critical information and resources on cultural responsiveness. The italicized sub bullets are for your information to guide the conversation while the numbered items are the actual agenda items that you share with the NS.

Agenda for Month 2 – CS version

1. Welcome and Review of Reflection Activity (10-15 min.)
    a. It is great to get this focused time with you again!
    b. How are you feeling about the first several weeks of your supervision activities?
    c. How have the conversations about feedback and collaboration gone with your trainees or other RBT supervisees?
    d. How has it gone with preparing agendas and keeping your supervision contacts on time? What was it like to self-monitor this way and what ideas do you have to revise your process?
    e. Let's look at the documentation for their accrued fieldwork hours to make sure everything is in good shape and accurate.

2. Review of self-assessment and draft goals (10-15 min.)
    a. Thank you for taking the time to complete these self-assessments and for your transparency and honesty.
        i. If your impressions seem to match their assessments, describe this to them and move on to b.
        ii. If your impression is that they may have overestimated or underestimated their skills, evaluate how confident you are that their assessment is suspect.
            1. If you are very confident because you previously served as a supervisor of theirs, explain that your impressions differ on some of the items and discuss the potential discrepancy that you may be seeing with respect to confidence and competence (i.e., one is too high or low with respect to the other).
            2. If you suspect that one or more of the items on the self-assessment are off but you have limited data to support this, explain that you would love to hear more about what led them to score item X the way that they did.
    b. Thank you for taking the time to draft these initial goals as well. Do you have any revisions or updates to those goals that you want to talk about before we choose topics?
    c. Discuss any areas in the foundational skills that are scored as areas of need and select two to three of those that are in alignment with their goals to cover in months 4, 5, and 6. If there are no foundational skills that are scored as areas of need, move on to the advanced skills and plan out those same months. Update your planning guide that is provided in Appendix A.

3. Plan for using a similar self-assessment and direct assessment approach with their trainee. (5 min.)
    a. You did a great job conducting a self-assessment on your supervisory skills. You can use the same approach with your trainee regarding their basic behavior analysis skills and core professional skills.
    b. Tell me how you are thinking about applying this strategy of self-assessment with your trainee. How will you introduce the topic of self-assessing and why it is important?
    c. Do you have a plan to directly assess skills to validate and supplement the self-assessment?

4. Discussion of importance of cultural responsiveness in supervision and practice (20-25 min.)

   a. *Review the concept of cultural responsiveness. Ask questions to explore their level of familiarity with the topic (e.g., Have you had any instruction related to cultural responsiveness? How familiar is this term to you? What are some other terms related to culture, inclusion, and diversity that you are familiar with? Are you aware that this term appears in the BACB Ethics Code for Behavior Analysts and the RBT Ethics Code (2.0)?).*

   b. *Explain the importance of culture in developing who we are and determining our biases. Introduce the activities that you would like them to complete to discuss next month. Go through the results of your self-reflection activity to illustrate various aspects of your background that are an important part of your history. Convey your interest in learning more about them in some of the same areas. Ask them to consider sharing the results of their own self-reflection with you in the next meeting if they feel comfortable doing so.*

   c. *Review the concept of cultural humility and power differentials. As the CS, you have an inherent power differential in your favor with the NS, just as they do with their new trainees and supervisees. Talk about the importance of recognizing that power differential and the criticality of actively behaving in ways that convey mutual respect and create brave/safe spaces for others. Without this, bi-directional feedback is unlikely to occur.*

5. Wrap up (3-5 mins.)

   a. *Review action items for each party*
   b. *Set the next meeting time and date*

Agenda to Share with NS 24 hours in advance

1. Welcome and Review of Reflection Activity. (10-15 min.)

2. Review of self-assessment and draft goals. (10-15 min.)

3. Plan for using self-assessment and direct assessment with trainee. (5 min.)

4. Discussion of importance of cultural responsiveness in supervision and practice. (20-25 min.)

5. Wrap up. (3-5 min.)

Welcome and Review of Reflection Activity

This agenda item gives you an opportunity to continue to build rapport with the NS. If you did not have any previous relationship, take a moment or two to ask a question that allows you to get to know them better as a person and a professional (e.g., How long have you been with your organization? Where did graduate school fit in for you – right after undergraduate, after working in the field for a while?). Remember to always lead with the relationship as you are modeling this approach for the NS.

You will also get the details about the supervision activities (i.e., preparation, meetings, and observations) the NS has completed this month. You should check in on how many contacts occurred with the trainee and/or supervisees and the extent to which each of those was planned and met the requirements of the BACB. You should double check the documentation and calculation of accrued hours for the month to catch any mistakes that might occur early and to help the NS plan needed follow-up tasks. Ask open-ended questions about how the various experiences went and how well the supervision time was managed. Several potential open-ended questions are provided in your detailed agenda to get you started. Since the NS has completed an activity to prepare them for this discussion and review, they should be able to readily answer these open-ended questions with detailed responses.

 ## Review of Self-Assessment and Goals

You will initiate a discussion with the NS about the importance of self-assessment as a supplement to ongoing direct observation assessment of skills. Describe that even when you have the opportunity to directly observe skills, a self-assessment provides information about that individual's ability to accurately observe and assess their own skills. Their self-assessment might seem highly consistent with direct observation data, an underestimate of skills compared to direct observation, or an overestimate of skills compared to direct observation. When you compare a self-assessment to direct evidence of skills, you are investigating the relationship between someone's competence (i.e., what they can actually do) and their confidence (i.e., what they feel about how well they do things). Discrepancy in either direction (i.e., overconfidence, excessive self-doubt) could be detrimental to learning and to ongoing practice.

You have access to the self-assessment completed by the NS, and you also have access to their initial draft of goals for the consulting experience. Review those carefully considering whether the self-assessment correlates with any other data you might have about the NS. You will make an initial determination about the correspondence between these two sets of data. If you identify a discrepancy, it is worth targeting that discrepancy (i.e., specifically covering self-observing and assessing) as part of your efforts during this year of consulting. If you do not have any other sources of data except the self-assessment, it is still worth discussing the importance of correspondence between competence and confidence in your meetings with the NS.

Ask various open-ended questions about skills and needs based on the information provided by the NS in their self-assessment. Consider an example: the self-assessment indicates that the NS has had coursework on behavioral skills training (BST) and has been taught skills via that approach, but has never created BST materials, taught someone else a skill using the BST, or taught someone else how to use BST. In this example you might ask questions that provide information about how fully the NS understands each component of BST and whether the BST they experienced was optimal (e.g., "What skill did you learn via BST?" "Did the trainer use a job aid, and if so, what was the job aid like?" "How many times did you have to rehearse with feedback until you met criterion?"). These questions might reveal that the prior BST did not include core components like a model or practice to criterion. In that case, you might want to include BST in your plan of targeted skills, focusing on explaining what components might have been missing and sharing examples of BST materials that could serve as a model for the NS's initial training efforts (e.g., a sample job aid, a data sheet for scoring rehearsal trials and guiding feedback until a mastery criterion is met).

Discuss any items in the foundational skills that are scored as areas of need and select two to three that are in alignment with the NS's goals to cover in months 4, 5, and 6 of your consulting efforts. It might be the case that there are no foundational skills that are scored as areas of need, particularly if your NS has been functioning as a BCaBA for a while providing training and supervisor to RBTs. If this is the case, have them show you a prior work sample and if the sample supports their self-assessment, move on to the advanced skills assessment (see Month 6 NS Workbook) and plan out those same months. Update your yearly planning guide that is provided in Appendix A and give a copy to the NS so that they can coordinate the monthly topics in your future meetings. In your discussion about assessment in general, convey to the NS the importance of assessing a broad array of skills that allow them to plan their curriculum and instruction during fieldwork (or ongoing RBT supervision). Of course, many items from the BACB Task List will be included in the skills that are assessed (e.g., preference assessment, direct instruction, contingencies). However, the curriculum developed by the NS for their trainees should focus heavily on the practical aspects of these topics (i.e., doing the procedures, selecting the conditions that are optimally suited to using that procedure, recognizing an instance of a given contingency) rather than the academic aspects of these topics that are typically taught and tested in academic courses (i.e., providing a textbook definition of a contingency, listing the components of a procedure).

BACB Task List Fifth Edition Item	Sample Academic Coursework Content	Sample Fieldwork Content
G-9 Use discrete-trial, free-operant, and naturalistic teaching arrangements	Listing the components of a discrete trial	Performing discrete trials accurately at a reasonable pace
F-5 Conduct preference assessments.	Identifying which preference assessment procedure was studied in several different articles	Performing multiple types of preference assessments accurately Selecting the type of preference assessment that is best suited to client circumstances
A-2 Explain the philosophical assumptions underlying the science of behavior analysis (e.g., selectionism, determinism, empiricism, parsimony, pragmatism).	Matching the core assumptions of a scientific framework to their definition and examples	Exhibiting skepticism in everyday activities Explaining why they need to take an experimental approach with a client and indicating which type of design is best suited to their circumstances

In addition to the BACB Task List, it is important to assess pivotal professional skills such as organization, time management, problem-solving, communication skills, and interpersonal relationship skills. The NS will often assess these skills based on direct observation during direct observation and supervision meetings (e.g., do they have everything that they need for the supervision, have they tracked their hours correctly, can they role-play touchy conversations effectively) with their trainee. However, it is still worth having any supervisee or trainee complete a self-assessment of these skills and common problems with these skills.

In LeBlanc, Sellers et al. (2020), a supervisor will find assessments and self-assessments for each of these skill sets in chapters 6, 7, 8, and 9. The NS will have been preparing for this discussion by creating an initial plan for assessing their trainee's skills and having the trainee self-assess. Review the plan during the consulting meeting and help the NS improve the plan as needed (e.g., suggest that the NS have the trainee complete the self-assessment for the BACB Task List created by Biagi and Tagg that is available in LeBlanc, Sellers et al., (2020). Make sure that the NS realizes that one single assessment or self-assessment is unlikely to suffice.

Discuss Culturally Responsive and Humble Practices

You have dual goals for this section of the agenda. First, you want to enhance the NS's understanding of cultural responsiveness and humility in their practice and their supervision. Many people are at least a little anxious with regard to differences and diversity. However, "while sometimes uncomfortable, diversity brings opportunities for learning, connection, and progress." (LeBlanc, Sellers et al., 2020, p. 43). You want to help this NS embrace the upcoming opportunities for learning that diversity will bring throughout their career. It is a given that they will serve clients, families, supervisees, and trainees who differ from them. Second, you want to explore any cultural differences between you and the NS to a) identify any potential factors that might influence your consulting relationship and b) model an approach that the NS can imitate when interacting with their own supervisees and trainees. "Cultural differences impact supervision whether the supervisor and supervisee are aware of it or not." (LeBlanc, Sellers et al., 2020, p. 43). When you explore cultural differences as a regular part of strengthening any supervisory relationship, you create proactive dialogue about the importance of culture in all aspects of life. There may well be unidentified cultural differences between you and the NS that become evident during the discussion. You should complete the Self-Reflection on Culturally Responsive and Humble Practices provided in Appendix B at the end of this workbook as a self-reflection to guide your discussion of your own cultural background and practices with the NS. Explain why you think this activity is important and that you are interested in learning more about them and any differences that may exist between the two of you. Assign them to complete it for the following meeting for continued discussion and model how to summarize results by telling them about your own results.

From the BACB Code (BACB, 2020)

1.07 Cultural Responsiveness and Diversity
Behavior analysts actively engage in professional development activities to acquire knowledge and skills related to cultural responsiveness and diversity. They evaluate their own biases and ability to address the needs of individuals with diverse needs/backgrounds (e.g., age, disability, ethnicity, gender expression/identity, immigration status, marital/relationship status, national origin, race, religion, sexual orientation, socioeconomic status). Behavior analysts also evaluate biases of their supervisees and trainees, as well as their supervisees' and trainees' ability to address the needs of individuals with diverse needs/backgrounds.

1.08 Nondiscrimination
Behavior analysts do not discriminate against others. They behave toward others in an equitable and inclusive manner regardless of age, disability, ethnicity, gender expression/identity, immigration status, marital/relationship status, national origin, race, religion, sexual orientation, socioeconomic status, or any other basis proscribed by law.

4.07 Incorporating and Addressing Diversity (see 1.05, 1.06, 1.07, 1.10)
During supervision and training, behavior analysts actively incorporate and address topics related to diversity (e.g., age, disability, ethnicity, gender expression/identity, immigration status, marital/ relationship status, national origin, race, religion, sexual orientation, socioeconomic status).

If this topic is relatively new to you, you might want to explore the following resources in advance of the Month 2 consultation meeting. You might also consider recommending some of these same resources to the NS as resources to explore their own cultural awareness:

1. Conners et al., (2019)
2. Conners & Capell (2020)
3. Fong et al. (2016)
4. LeBlanc, Sellers, et al. (2020) Chapter 4
5. Wright (2019)

The term "cultural responsiveness" refers to practices that are informed by and consistent with appreciation and respect for diversity and its many intersections (LeBlanc, Sellers et al. 2020). Culturally responsive practices emphasize the importance of assessing and understanding your own cultural experiences so that you become more aware of the factors that afford you privilege and influence your way of seeing the world. They also focus on the importance of learning from, appreciating, and taking into consideration the cultural experiences of others, whether they are similar to or different from yours. In addition, when differences exist such that clients or supervisees have social, cultural, and linguistic needs to succeed either in therapy or supervision, you take action to honor and meet those needs (LeBlanc, Sellers, et al., 2020). A culturally responsive supervisor or consultant reflects on the influences of culture on their behavior, creates a welcoming environment for supervisees and trainees to behave authentically with respect to their differences, and adjust their behavior to respect the cultural preferences and needs of others.

Recent discussions use the concept of "cultural humility" (Wright, 2019) which places an emphasis on understanding the power differentials that exist in most professional relationships and the benefits of being humble regarding cultural knowledge (Fisher-Bourne et al., 2015 Hook et al., 2013). A culturally humble supervisor or consultant can admit what they do not know and to actively seek to understand and learn. There is an inherent power differential between the supervisee and supervisor (in your case between the NS and you as the consultant). This power differential may be increased by other cultural differences that exist.

In your discussion with the NS, explore strategies that they might use in their ongoing supervisory activities to show respect for their supervisees and to convey safety in the supervisory relationship. For example, they might inquire about pronouns and use those pronouns accurately, make note of religious days of importance for the other person, and use culturally diverse examples in any scenarios and materials that they use with their supervisees.

You might consider having the NS complete Chapter 4, Activity 1 from LeBlanc, Sellers et al. (2020) which is a cultural awareness interview. This gives them the opportunity to reflect on their own culture as well as to discuss culture in interviews with each other. This activity may be particularly useful for NSs who have not had the opportunity to function independently as a BCBA for very long. In addition, it may be useful to ask the NS to complete an assessment of privilege using one of the available online tools or Activity 2 of Chapter 4 from LeBlanc, Sellers et al. (2020). Finally, ask the NS to complete the *Self-Reflection on Culturally Responsive and Humble Practices* provided in Appendix B. They will likely need to take this reflection activity away with them, so plan to continue your discussion of this topic in Month 3.

Wrap Up
....

You are continuing to provide a model of well-run meetings, which could be a new experience for some individuals. You are also modeling using open ended questions throughout your meetings to keep the focus of building a strong, bi-directional relationship based on shared power in the forefront. You have now begun to individualize your plan for this NS to help them meet their goals for the experience. We hope you have also found it useful to hone your knowledge and discourse about three important topics: 1) the value of effective meetings, 2) the value of assessment activities in individualized supervision, and 3) the value of self-reflection and humility in cultural responsiveness. You are providing a tremendous service to this NS, and we hope this workbook helps to repay that service with new and refined knowledge and skills.

 Reflection and Goal Evaluation

After you have completed the Month 2 consultation, reflect on the goals for this month and evaluate how well your efforts met those goals.

- Maintain and strengthen your relationship with the NS
- Review outcomes of first meeting with trainees
- Review how the first month went
- Review trainee documentation to ensure accuracy
- Discuss the results of the NS self-assessment implications for months 4-6
- Discuss the plan for self-assessment and assessment with trainees
- Discuss core features of culturally responsive and humble supervisory and clinical practices
- Identify any potential cultural differences that could impact your relationship with the NS

You may want to send a follow up email thanking the NS for their participation in the meeting and checking up on any items from the agenda that were not completed or any goals that were not met. Make any notes from your reflections here and use these notes to help you prepare for Month 3:

_____
_____
_____
_____
_____
_____
_____
_____

Month 3
Curricular Roadmap and Competencies

Goals for Upcoming Meeting

- Continue to strengthen the relationship with the NS.
- Review outcomes of Month-2 supervision activities with trainees and documentation.
- Review proposed strategies for soliciting feedback.
- Review workload assessment that the NS repeated and help to problem-solve if any problems are detected.
- Revisit the topic of cultural awareness and review the results of the self-reflection activities.
- Support the NS in making the months 3-11 plan of target skills and competencies for their trainees.
- Turn over agenda planning to the NS.

The NS has now been providing fieldwork supervision for at least two full months with their trainee as well as several contacts with other RBT supervisees. They should be regularly creating agendas for their contacts, providing feedback, and documenting their supervision along with the fieldwork hours accrual with their trainee. If you are still seeing issues with documentation when you check this month, it may be time for a discussion about the importance of accurate documentation and the need to review the *BCBA Handbook* again.

They have also been diligently preparing for their Month 3 meeting with you. Their workbook prompts them to engage in several tasks that will allow the two of you to make the most of your limited time together. These items will make up much of the content of your meeting with them. In addition, you will turn over the agenda preparation to the NS for the remaining months unless you have detected any performance issues related to creating effective agendas and running meetings. Each item on your agenda is described below to help you prepare for the meeting.

1. **Reflection on the supervisory contacts for the month and workload assessment**. The NS should be in a great position to give you a concise update on what has occurred in their supervision meetings and observations, highlighting any specific points of celebration or concern. They should also have trainee documentation to show you so that you can identify any errors. Review the documentation carefully and determine whether you need to continue to review it every month (i.e., the documentation contains repeated errors or new ones) or not (i.e., no errors detected for at least two months). The NS should have reviewed and potentially revised the goals they originally drafted based on the discussion last meeting. They may or may not send those to you in advance of the meeting. There may or may not be any need to update the plan you made in the last meeting. The NS

will also have completed the Workload Assessment activity again and compared it to the one completed in the Getting Ready section. We have provided the activity at the end of this chapter for your reference. They should have emailed or shared the results with you in advance of the next meeting. Be prepared to address any concerns that have arisen in the meeting so that you can support the NS if they are becoming overwhelmed. Sample questions are provided in your agenda to guide this discussion.

2. **Review strategies for soliciting feedback from trainees**. The NS should have proposed strategies for how they plan to solicit feedback from their trainees. They will likely have a form that they should use with the trainee in months 3, 6, 9, and 12. Their workbook included a sample and we have provided the same one at the end of this chapter for your reference. They should be able to describe how the feedback will be obtained (e.g., in-person discussion, completing the form on the computer and sending, printing and filling out and dropping in a box or giving to someone who will then pass them to you, completing an online anonymous option like Survey Monkey). They should also have a plan for how they will introduce this to the trainee (e.g., "This is a chance for me to improve my supervisory skills, which I value greatly"). Sample questions are provided in the agenda to guide this discussion.

3. **Self-reflection and self-assessment related to culture and cultural responsiveness**. The NS should have completed the activities that you provided last month. Take this opportunity to ask how their thoughts about culture may have shifted since that discussion (e.g., more thoughts about it, realizations, insights). Ask if they have obtained any results or insights from their self-assessment and self-reflection that they would like to discuss.

4. **Review of trainee self-assessment and assessment activities and initial thoughts on goals**. The NS should describe the results of the assessments they have completed with their trainees, focusing on whether they have identified any areas of significant concern or disconnects between the results (i.e., between how they and your trainee evaluated the trainee's skills). If needed, role-play conversations for discussing the results with the trainee. The NS should have the beginnings of a plan for a curricular roadmap for their trainee based on their trainee's skills assessment and self-assessment. It may need more details or changes in priorities, so be prepared to offer them feedback and suggestions in a positive, supportive manner. You may need to guide them to simplify their plan or to be more specific with their language or criteria. Sample questions are provided in the agenda to guide this discussion.

5. **Turn over the agenda responsibilities to the NS**. Thus far, you have been creating the agendas for your consultation meetings and the NS has been creating agendas for their supervision activities with their trainees and monitoring the accuracy of their time estimates. The NS has also been teaching their trainees how to create agendas. Ask if their trainees are ready to take over all or some of the agenda planning for their supervision meetings. If the NS says it is going well, ask if they have officially turned over that responsibility or not. Identify a month when that might happen if it has not already happened. If there is a concern, talk about it and help them problem solve. That is, if there is a deficit on the part of their trainee, you want to help them see this as an opportunity to teach and support rather than avoid and accommodate. You also want to turn over responsibility for creating the agendas for the consultation meetings to the NS. The NS should create the agendas for Months

4-12 of the consulting meetings using the plan that you jointly created in a prior month. They should also feel free to modify that plan, in consultation with you, as needs arise. Create an explicit expectation that they should send you an agenda at least 24-48 hours prior to your next consultation meeting and all subsequent meetings. Sample questions are provided in the agenda to guide the discussion.

Here is an agenda for this month's consultation meeting. The italicized sub-bullets are for your information to guide the conversation. The numbered items are the actual agenda items that you share with the NS.

Agenda for Month 3—CS version

1. Welcome, Review of Your Supervision Activities, Goals, and Workload Assessment (10 min.)
       a. *It is great to get this focused time with you again!*
       b. *How are you feeling about the first few months of your supervision activities?*
       c. *How do you feel about the degree of collaboration and bi-directional feedback with your trainees or other RBT supervisees?*
       d. *How has it gone with preparing agendas and keeping your supervision contacts on time?*
       e. *Let's look at the documentation for your trainees' accrued fieldwork hours to make sure everything is in good shape and accurate.*
       f. *Have you identified any revisions to your goals?*
       g. *What does your updated workload assessment tell you about your capacity to provide supervision? Are you feeling good/overwhelmed/apprehensive about this? Let's identify one thing that you could do if the workload feels like it doesn't allow adequate time for supervision.*

2. Review of plan to seek feedback on supervision (5 min.)
       a. *How will you seek feedback from your trainee on the quality of your supervision, their preferences, and the effects of your supervision?*

3. Review of culturally responsive and humble practices activity and ongoing discussions with trainees (10 min.)
       a. *Were you able to complete the activities designed to help you explore your culture, your privilege, and whether your practices are culturally responsive?*
       b. *What insights would you like to share?*
       c. *How will you translate this activity into something that can enhance*
          - *Your relationship with your trainees; and*
          - *Your efforts to teach your trainees about cultural humility?*

4. Review the results of the trainee self-assessment and direct observation (10 min.)
       a. *How did the assessment process go with your trainee?*
       b. *What are your thoughts on agreement or disagreement between the self-assessment and any of your direct observations? If disagreement, how will you target accuracy in your curricular roadmap?*

5. Create the curricular roadmap for the trainee (10 min.)
   a. Let's review the ideas you had for goals and specific skills for your trainee.
   b. Follow-up questions:
      - Should this one go earlier or later in your roadmap?
      - How confident do you feel in targeting the skills early in your roadmap? Is there something you would feel more confident targeting early on?

6. Transition of agenda responsibilities (5 min.)
   a. Let's talk about how it is going in your discussions about agendas with your trainees. Have they read any articles or chapters on that?
   b. If not, suggest LeBlanc, Sellers et al. (2020) or LeBlanc and Nosik (2019).
   c. It is important for your trainees to feel like they have some responsibility and control over their fieldwork experience and that they can make the most of their supervision. Turning over some or all of the responsibility for initial agenda preparation helps with this.
   d. Do you feel like your trainees are ready to take over initial agenda planning for their supervision meetings? Have you already turned over this responsibility? Let's identify when this transition might occur.
   e. I would like to have the same transition occur with our consultation meetings. Could you (NS) please create the agendas for the rest of our consultation meetings using the resources in your workbook and the plan that we developed for you? Here is a copy of the plan. Of course, this plan can be flexible if some urgent need arises. We will also do more assessment to develop the plan for the last six months.
   f. Please send the agenda at least 24-48 hours in advance of our meetings so that I am prepared to be a resource for you in our meetings. I will also add items to your draft agenda periodically.

7. Wrap up (3-5 min.)
   a. Review action items for each party.
   b. Set the next meeting time and date.

Agenda to Share with NS 24 hours in advance

1. Welcome, Review of Your Supervision Activities, Goals, and Workload Assessment. (10 min.)

2. Review your plan for soliciting feedback on supervision. (5 min.)

3. Review of culturally responsive and humble practices activity. (10 min.)

4. Review the results of your trainee self-assessment and your observations. (10 min.)

5. Create a curricular roadmap for supervision with your trainee. (10 min.)

6. Transitioning responsibility for agenda preparation. (5 min.)

7. Wrap up. (3-5 min.)

 ## Reflection and Goal Evaluation

After you have completed the Month-3 consultation, reflect on the goals for this month and evaluate how well your efforts met those goals. Remember, the goals were as follows:

- Maintain and strengthen your relationship with the NS.
- Review how supervision is going with trainees and review documentation to ensure accuracy.
- Review the proposed strategies for soliciting feedback.
- Review the workload assessment that the NS repeated and help to problem-solve if any problems are detected.
- Revisit the topic of cultural awareness and review the results of the self-reflection activities.
- Support the NS in making the months 3-11 plan of target skills and competencies for their trainees.
- Turn over agenda planning to the NS.

You may want to send a follow-up email thanking the NS for their participation in the meeting and checking up on any items from the agenda that were not completed or any goals that were not met. Make any notes from your reflections here and use these notes to help you prepare for Month 4. Make sure that you make calendar time to carry out any tasks your agreed to in the meeting (e.g., sending articles or other resources, reviewing any documents the NS provided to you).

_____
_____
_____

Workload Assessment Month-3 Template from the NS Workbook

Task	Average Weekly Time Requirement	Facilitators	Barriers
Client caseload management			
RBT caseload			
BCaBA caseload			
Trainee caseload			
Administrative responsibilities			
Other duties			
Total average weekly work hours			

Month 3 Appendix A—From the NS Workbook

Soliciting Formal Feedback from Trainee

Always = 3   Usually = 2   Never = 1

If an item is not applicable strike through the scoring numbers and skip it. Place an "X" in the "Specific Feedback" column if you provided specific feedback about this item in the notes section.

Item	Score	Specific Feedback?
1. Supervisor is timely (e.g., arriving for meetings, meeting due dates).	3 2 1	
2. Supervisor follows through on tasks.	3 2 1	
3. Supervisor provides clear expectations of tasks and due dates.	3 2 1	
4. Supervisor creates a collaborative relationship.	3 2 1	
5. Supervisor demonstrates culturally responsive and humble practices.	3 2 1	
6. Supervisor is actively engaged in meetings and observations.	3 2 1	
7. Supervisor treats me with respect and dignity.	3 2 1	
8. Supervisor treats mistakes as learning opportunities.	3 2 1	
9. Supervisor provides the opportunity to ask questions and provides full answers.	3 2 1	
10. Supervisor solicits feedback regularly.	3 2 1	
11. Supervisor engages in high-quality, feedback-reception skills.	3 2 1	
12. Supervisor implements feedback that I have provided.	3 2 1	
13. Supervisor delivers high-quality feedback (e.g., behavior specific).	3 2 1	
14. Supervisor reviews written products (e.g., reports, protocols, emails).	3 2 1	
15. Supervisor documents activities and feedback.	3 2 1	
16. Supervisor implements high-quality instruction (e.g., BST).	3 2 1	
17. Supervisor uses a competency-based approach to teaching me.	3 2 1	
18. Supervisor addresses behavior-analytic content and items from the BACB Task List.	3 2 1	
19. Supervisor covers ethics content.	3 2 1	
20. Supervisor includes other content linked to success as a clinician and future supervisor (e.g., organization and time management, interpersonal communication, problem-solving).	3 2 1	
21. Supervisor makes space for addressing self-care and stress management.	3 2 1	
22. Supervisor facilitates my ability to make clinical decisions.	3 2 1	
23. Supervisor facilitates my professional development.	3 2 1	
TOTAL:		

List three things that your supervisor consistently does well:

1. _____

2. _____

3. _____

List three things on which my supervisor could improve (this could be increasing consistency or quality, doing more of something, doing less of something, adding in something they currently are not doing):

1. _____

2. _____

3. _____

Item Specific Feedback

Item Number	Feedback

Month-to-Month Guides
The Individualized Plan

The topics to be addressed in Months 4–6 were selected by you and the NS based on the self-reflection and self-assessment activities of the NS and your own observations of the NS. In Month 6, the NS will repeat the Foundational Skills Assessment and will complete the Advanced Skills Assessment to identify the content to address in Months 7–11. The NS will simultaneously use a similar plan for their trainees. Planning is important but it is also important to be flexible and respond to emerging needs that are identified by the NS in their reflections, in your evaluation based on you consulting sessions, and any urgent needs that arise with the NS's trainees. If needed, spend more than one month on a topic or jump ahead to a topic that has suddenly become pressing (e.g., crucial-conversations topic was scheduled for Month 8, but in Month 5 you realize you need to have one with your trainee now).

The following section provides outlines for Month 4–11 for you to plan your activities with your NS based on the drafted roadmaps and goals. Each month's template contains a standard outline for the specific topics and skills to be addressed that month with the NS. It will also include suggestions for questions and topics related to maturation as a supervisor and detection of stress and burnout. Included is a list of reminders for each month about review of specific activities that the NS should have completed (e.g., reassessing skills, repeated workload assessment, soliciting formal feedback from trainees). The NS will be preparing the agendas for these meetings, so make sure that you are prompting them to send those in advance so that you will know if the topic has been changed from the original plan.

Month 4

Goals for Upcoming Meeting

- Continue to strengthen the relationship with the NS.
- Review outcomes of Month-3 supervision activities with trainees and documentation.
- Provide feedback on the agenda that the NS creates for the meeting.
- Cover the Specific Skill topic that you and the NS selected for month 4.
- Support the NS with any issues that are arising in their supervisory activities.

You and the NS selected a specific topic to cover for their professional development in Month 4 and you should have tracked this in the chart that you created. The NS may also have selected a different skill for their trainees. The NS is now responsible for creating the agenda and sending it to you in advance. Review that agenda and provide any feedback on it prior to the meeting.

Check the yearly planning guide/roadmap. What is the topic for this month?

_____

Preparation

- Review the Specific Skill entry for that topic.
- Prepare open-ended questions that can guide the discussion about that topic (e.g., "What seemed most useful from this section of your workbook?" "What did you have questions about?").
- Reflect on your own skills in this area using the prompts provided in the skill-specific section. Prepare to discuss at least one of those reflections.
- If you are aware of resources other than the ones listed in the Specific Skill section, share those with the NS and describe how you have found them useful.

Reflection and Goal Evaluation

How well did you meet the following goals?

- Maintain and strengthen your relationship with the NS.
- Review how supervision is going with trainees and review documentation to ensure accuracy.
- Provide feedback on the agenda.
- Provide support for any issues in supervision.
- Cover the Specific Skill topic.

Notes: _____

Month 5

GOALS FOR UPCOMING MEETING

- Continue to strengthen the relationship with the NS.
- Review outcomes of Month-4 supervision activities with trainees and documentation.
- Cover the Specific Skill topic that you and the NS selected for month 5.
- Support the NS with any issues that are arising in their supervisory activities.

You and the NS selected a specific topic to cover for their professional development in Month 5 and you should have tracked this in the chart that you created. Something may have come up that led the NS to change topics. If so, they should have notified you in advance and reflected the change in the upcoming agenda.

Check the yearly planning guide/roadmap and any correspondence from the NS. What is the topic for this month?

_____

Preparation

- Review the Specific Skill entry for that topic.
- Prepare open-ended questions that can guide the discussion about that topic (e.g., "What seemed most useful from this section of your workbook?" "What did you have questions about?").
- Reflect on your own skills in this area using the prompts in the skills-specific section. Prepare to discuss at least one of those reflections.
- If you are aware of resources other than the ones listed in the Specific Skill section, share those with the NS and describe how you have found them useful.
- Prompt the NS to celebrate that they have now been supervising for at least 4-5 months. Ask what has been the most rewarding experience so far? Ask how you can better support them. Ask open-ended questions instead of yes/no questions to facilitate a robust conversation.

Reflection and Goal Evaluation

How well did you meet the following goals?

- Maintain and strengthen your relationship with the NS.
- Review how supervision is going with trainees and review documentation to ensure accuracy.
- Provide support for any issues in supervision.
- Cover the Specific Skill topic.

Notes: _____

Month 6

Goals for Upcoming Meeting

- Continue to strengthen the relationship with the NS.
- Review outcomes of Month-5 supervision activities with trainees and documentation.
- Review the updated workload assessment and provide any support that is required.
- Review the results of the NS's Foundational Supervision Skills reassessment to evaluate progress. The NS should have identified areas where they have improved and areas for continued growth.
- Review the results of the NS's Advanced Supervision Skills Assessment and complete the rest of the roadmap chart to identify topics for months 7-11 for the NS and their trainees.
- Cover the Specific Skill topic that you and the NS selected for month 6.
- Support the NS with any issues that are arising in their supervisory activities.

Month 6 focuses heavily on reassessment and development or revision of the curricular roadmap for your consulting activities and the NS's supervisory activities. The tools from their Workbook are provided below for your reference. You likely also selected a specific topic to cover for their professional development in Month 6 and you should have tracked this in the yearly planning guide/NS's roadmap.

Check the yearly planning guide/roadmap and any correspondence from the NS. What is the topic for this month?

_____

Preparation

- Review the Specific Skill entry for that topic.
- Prepare open-ended questions that can guide the discussion about that topic (e.g., "What seemed most useful from this section of your workbook?" "What did you have questions about?").
- Reflect on your own skills in this area using the prompts provided in the chart. Prepare to discuss at least one of those reflections.
- If you are aware of resources other than the ones listed in the Specific Skill section, share those with the NS and describe how you have found them useful.
- If the NS sends their reassessment in advance, review it and be prepared to discuss your thoughts.
- If the NS sends any information about their assessment activities with their trainees, review it in advance.

Reflection and Goal Evaluation

How well did you meet the following goals?

- Maintain and strengthen your relationship with the NS.
- Review how supervision is going with trainees and review documentation to ensure accuracy.
- Review the reassessment and advanced skills assessment and integrate the results into your plan for future consultation meetings.
- Provide support for any issues in supervision.
- Cover the Specific Skill topic.

Notes: _____

Month 7

> **Goals for Upcoming Meeting**
> - Continue to strengthen the relationship with the NS.
> - Review outcomes of Month-6 supervision activities with trainees and documentation.
> - Cover the Specific Skill topic that you and the NS selected for month 7.
> - Support the NS with any issues that are arising in their supervisory activities.

You and the NS selected a specific topic to cover for their professional development in Month 7 and you should have tracked this in the yearly planning guide/roadmap. Something may have come up that led the NS to change topics. If so, they should have notified you in advance.

Check the yearly planning guide/roadmap and any correspondence from the NS. What is the topic for this month?

_____

Preparation

- Review the Specific Skill entry for that topic:
- Prepare open-ended questions that can guide the discussion about that topic (e.g., "What seemed most useful from this section of your workbook?" "What did you have questions about?").
- Reflect on your own skills in this area using the prompts provided in the skills-specific section. Prepare to discuss at least one of those reflections.
- If you are aware of resources other than the ones listed in the Specific Skill section, share those with the NS and describe how you have found them useful.
- Ask the NS to reflect on the strategies they are using during direct observation sessions to maintain a dual and balanced focus on 1) improving client services, and 2) improving the supervisee's or trainee's repertoires.

Reflection and Goal Evaluation

How well did you meet the following goals?

- Maintain and strengthen your relationship with the NS.
- Review how supervision is going with trainees and review documentation to ensure accuracy.
- Provide support for any issues in supervision.
- Cover the Specific Skill topic.

Notes:

Month 8

Goals for Upcoming Meeting

- Continue to strengthen the relationship with the NS.
- Review outcomes of Month-7 supervision activities with trainees and documentation.
- Review the Burnout Assessment that the NS completed.
- Cover the Specific Skill topic that you and the NS selected for Month 8.
- Support the NS with any issues that are arising in their supervisory activities.

You and the NS are well over halfway through your consulting relationship and the NS has been supervising for quite a while. It is important to talk about burnout and the importance of periodically self-assessing for burnout. The NS has an assessment in their Workbook that they should complete prior to this month's consulting meeting. We have provided the assessment for your reference. You may also want to complete it for yourself. Prepare to discuss your results and those of the NS. Take the opportunity to contextualize burnout as something that can be discussed openly and that can be addressed with a plan if necessary. If you or the NS need support with this topic, see Chapter 12 in LeBlanc, Sellers et al. (2020), the resources listed at the end of the burnout assessment, and the Specific Topic section on self-care. In addition, you and the NS selected a specific topic to cover for their professional development in Month 8 and you should have tracked this in the yearly planning guide/roadmap. Something may have come up that led the NS to change topics. If so, they should have notified you in advance.

Check the yearly planning guide/roadmap and any correspondence from the NS. What is the topic for this month?

Preparation

- Review and potentially complete the burnout assessment for yourself:
- If the NS sends you their results from the burnout assessment in advance, review those results in advance.
- Review the Specific Skill entry for that topic.
- Prepare open-ended questions that can guide the discussion about that topic (e.g., "What seemed most useful from this section of your workbook?" "What did you have questions about?").
- Reflect on your own skills in this area using the prompts provided in the skills-specific section. Prepare to discuss at least one of those reflections.
- If you are aware of resources other than the ones listed in the Specific Skill section, share those with the NS and describe how you have found them useful.

Reflection and Goal Evaluation

How well did you meet the following goals?

- Maintain and strengthen your relationship with the NS.
- Review how supervision is going with trainees and review documentation to ensure accuracy.
- Lead an open, honest discussion about burnout and the results of the burnout assessment(s).
- Provide support for any issues in supervision.
- Cover the Specific Skill topic.

Notes:

Month 8 Burnout Self-Assessment

The Copenhagen Burnout Inventory (CPI)   Kristensen et al. (2005)

Instructions: Review the definitions of the three categories below, then score each question by entering the score value (e.g., 100, 75, 50, 25, 0) in the scoring column.

From Kristensen et al. (p. 197, 2005):

> *"Personal burnout is the degree of physical and psychological fatigue and exhaustion experienced by the person."*

> *Client-related burnout:* *"The degree of physical and psychological fatigue and exhaustion that is perceived by the person as related to his/her work with clients."*

> *Work-related burnout:* *"The degree of physical and psychological fatigue and exhaustion that is perceived by the person as related to his/her work."*

Items	Always or to a very high degree (100)	Often or to a high degree (75)	Sometimes or somewhat (50)	Seldom or to a low degree (25)	Never or almost never; to a very low degree (0)
Personal Burnout					
How often do you feel tired?					
How often are you physically exhausted?					
How often are you emotionally exhausted?					
How often do you think, "I can't take it anymore"?					
How often do you feel worn out?					
How often do you feel weak and susceptible to illness?					
Scoring Category Totals:					
Personal Burnout Total:					

Items	Always or to a very high degree (100)	Often or to a high degree (75)	Sometimes or somewhat (50)	Seldom or to a low degree (25)	Never or almost never; to a very low degree (0)
Work-Related Burnout					
Do you feel worn out at the end of the working day?					
Are you exhausted in the morning at the thought of another day at work?					
Do you feel that every working hour is tiring for you?					
Do you have enough energy for family and friends during leisure time?					
Is your work emotionally exhausting?					
Does your work frustrate you?					
Do you feel burnt out because of your work?					
Scoring Category Totals:					
Work-Related Burnout Total:					
Client-Related Burnout					
Do you find it hard to work with clients?					
Does it drain your energy to work with clients?					
Do you find it frustrating to work with clients?					
Do you feel that you give more than you get back when you work with clients?					
Are you tired of working with clients?					
Do you sometimes wonder how long you will be able to continue working with clients?					
Scoring Category Totals:					
Client-Related Burnout Total:					

FINAL SCORE: _____

The higher the total score, the greater the degree of burnout. Review the total scores for each category to identify if the level of burnout is consistent across all three or if it is higher in one of the categories. Work to identify strategies to address the effects of burnout for yourself or your trainees in the workplace and our personal lives. A number of journal articles published by behavior analysts outline and describe strategies to engage in active self-care and self-compassion practices to work toward achieving a healthy work-life balance and a sustained career. Many of the articles include descriptions of specific activities and practices, as well as robust resources (e.g., self-care assessments, recommended actions, books, web applications) to support you in your endeavors. Here are a few to get you started:

Self-Care and Burnout Specific Articles

Coyne, L. W., Gould, E. R., Grimaldi, M., Wilson, K. G., Baffuto, G., & Biglan, A. (2021). First things first: Parent psychological flexibility and self-compassion during COVID-19. *Behavior Analysis in Practice*, 14(4), 1092-1098.

Fiebig, J. H., Gould, E. R., Ming, S., & Watson, R. A. (2020). An invitation to act on the value of self-care: Being a whole person in all that you do. *Behavior Analysis in Practice*, 13(3), 559–567.

Slowiak, J. M., & De Longchamp, A. C. (2021). Self-care strategies and job-crafting practices among behavior analysts: Do they predict perceptions of work–life balance, work engagement, and burnout? *Behavior Analysis in Practice*, Advanced online publication. https://doi.org/10.1007/s40617-021-00570-y

Month 9

Goals for Upcoming Meeting

- Continue to strengthen the relationship with the NS.
- Review outcomes of Month-8 supervision activities with trainees and documentation.
- Review the workload reassessment completed by the NS.
- Cover the Specific Skill topic that you and the NS selected for Month 9.
- Support the NS with any issues that are arising in their supervisory activities.

The NS should complete another workload reassessment this month. The blank form is provided below for your reference. In addition, you and the NS selected a specific topic to cover for their professional development in Month 9 and you should have tracked this in the yearly planning guide/roadmap. Something may have come up that led the NS to change topics. If so, they should have notified you in advance.

Check the yearly planning guide/roadmap and any correspondence from the NS. What is the topic for this month?

_____

Preparation

- Review the Specific Skill entry for that topic.
- Prepare open-ended questions that can guide the discussion about that topic (e.g., "What seemed most useful from this section of your workbook?" "What did you have questions about?").
- Reflect on your own skills in this area using the prompts provided in the skills-specific section. Prepare to discuss at least one of those reflections.
- If you are aware of resources other than the ones listed in the Specific Skill section, share those with the NS and describe how you have found them useful.
- Reflect on strategies you have used to manage changes in your workload and prepare to discuss these strategies with the NS, particularly if they seem to be struggling to manage their workload.

 **Reflection and Goal Evaluation**

How well did you meet the following goals?

- Maintain and strengthen your relationship with the NS.
- Review how supervision is going with trainees and review documentation to ensure accuracy.
- Reviewed the workload reassessment and discussed strategies with the NS.
- Provide support for any issues in supervision.
- Cover the Specific Skill topic.

Notes: _____
_____
_____
_____
_____
_____
_____
_____
_____
_____
_____
_____
_____
_____
_____
_____
_____
_____
_____
_____

NS Workload Assessment Month 9

Task	Average Weekly Time Requirement	Facilitators	Barriers
Client caseload management			
RBT caseload			
BCaBA caseload			
Trainee caseload			
Administrative responsibilities			
Other duties			
Total average weekly work hours			

Month 10

> **Goals for Upcoming Meeting**
> - Continue to strengthen the relationship with the NS.
> - Review outcomes of Month-9 supervision activities with trainees and documentation.
> - Cover the Specific Skill topic that you and the NS selected for Month 10.
> - Support the NS with any issues that are arising in their supervisory activities.

You and the NS selected a specific topic to cover for their professional development in Month 10 and you should have tracked this in the yearly planning guide/roadmap. Something may have come up that led the NS to change topics. If so, they should have notified you in advance.

Check the yearly planning guide/roadmap and any correspondence from the NS. What is the topic for this month?

_____

Preparation

- Review the Specific Skill entry for that topic.
- Prepare open-ended questions that can guide the discussion about that topic (e.g., "What seemed most useful from this section of your workbook?" "What did you have questions about?).
- Reflect on your own skills in this area using the prompts provided in the skills-specific section. Prepare to discuss at least one of those reflections.
- If you are aware of resources other than the ones listed in the Specific Skill section, share those with the NS and describe how you have found them useful.
- Reflect on a Specific Skill topic that could be added to the Workbooks and ask the NS to nominate a topic as well during your meeting. Email the suggestion to us at linda@lbehavioral.com. We will be adding new content periodically and we will add your topic to our actions list.

Reflection and Goal Evaluation

How well did you meet the following goals? The goals were as follows:

- Maintain and strengthen your relationship with the NS.
- Review how supervision is going with trainees and review documentation to ensure accuracy.
- Provide support for any issues in supervision.
- Cover the Specific Skill topic.
- Identify other useful Skill topics.

Notes: _____

Month 11

> **Goals for Upcoming Meeting**
> - Continue to strengthen the relationship with the NS.
> - Review outcomes of Month-10 supervision activities with trainees and documentation.
> - Cover the Specific Skill topic that you and the NS selected for Month 11.
> - Support the NS with any issues that are arising in their supervisory activities.

You and the NS selected a specific topic to cover for their professional development in Month 10 and you should have tracked this in the yearly planning guide/roadmap. Something may have come up that led the NS to change topics. If so, they should have notified you in advance.

Check the yearly planning guide/roadmap and any correspondence from the NS. What is the topic for this month?

Preparation

- Review the Specific Skill entry for that topic.
- Prepare open-ended questions that can guide the discussion about that topic (e.g., "What seemed most useful from this section of your workbook?" "What did you have questions about?").
- Reflect on your own skills in this area using the prompts provided in the skills-specific section. Prepare to discuss at least one of those reflections.
- If you are aware of resources other than the ones listed in the Specific Skill section, share those with the NS and describe how you have found them useful.
- Reflect on the past 10 months of consulting. How have you (CS) grown? How have you seen the NS grow? Be prepared to describe this to the NS.

Reflection and Goal Evaluation

How well did you meet the following goals? The goals were as follows:

- Maintain and strengthen your relationship with the NS.
- Review how supervision is going with trainees and review documentation to ensure accuracy.
- Provide support for any issues in supervision.
- Cover the Specific Skill topic.
- Reflect on growth and change.

Notes: _____
_____
_____
_____
_____

Month 12
Facilitating Effective Professional Development Planning

> **Goals for Upcoming Meeting**
> - Review the NS's progress over the past 11 months and any evolution in their values.
> - Support the NS in planning for their continued professional development.
> - Review the progress of the NS's trainees as a means of evaluating the NS's supervision.
> - Celebrate, express gratitude, and discuss if there will be any ongoing connection with the NS.

WOW! You and your NS have made it!

Take a few deep breaths, drop your shoulders away from your ears, and take a moment to appreciate this moment. You now have eleven full months of consultation and mentoring with the NS. Because you took a planful approach, these past months have likely allowed you to provide the NS with valuable experiences and lessons in how to establish strong supervisory repertoires. This last month with your NS is all about reflecting on the past year, planning for the remaining time that you have with them, and preparing them for independence and career sustainability once you are no longer consulting with them.

The NS will have completed a new version of the Values Identification Activity (below) and compared it to the one completed early in the consulting relationship. They will also reflect on any changes in their practices with respect to cultural responsiveness and humility. They will be prepared to review and discuss these with you. They will also have reassessed burnout using the same assessment as in Month 8. If burnout was a concern in Month 8 and you helped the NS develop a plan, ask about how it is going and if there has been any improvement.

Preparation

- Reflect on the progress that you have seen in the NS and any areas in which you hope they will commit to continued development.
- If the NS sends you their repeat assessment of Foundational and Advanced Supervision Skills and draft goals before your meeting, review the results and be prepared to suggest areas for continued development.
- Reflect on any benefits you may have experienced as a result of consulting to the NS and be prepared to share those with the NS.
- Reflect on strategies that you have used to facilitate your own professional development while practicing independently and consider sharing with the NS.

Reflection and Goal Evaluation

How well did you meet the following goals?

- Review the NS's progress over the past 11 months and any evolution in their values.
- Support the NS in planning for their continued professional development.
- Review the progress of the NS's trainees as a means of evaluating the NS's supervision.
- Celebrate, express gratitude, and discuss if there will be any ongoing connection with the NS.

Notes:

NS Values-Identification Activity

Domain	Value	Example of Behaving Consistently with this Value	Strategy for Conveying this Value to Your Trainee
Practice			
Supervision			

CONGRATULATIONS, you amazing CS!

We hope that this workbook, and the companion workbook your NS may have been using have been helpful in putting some structure to your first year of consulting for NS(s). We hope that the material highlighted how critical high-quality supervision is, and how the repertoires needed to be successful go way beyond the BACB Task List and behavior-analytic knowledge and skills. We invite you to reflect on the gift that you have given to your NS, their trainees, their clients, their trainee's future trainees, and the profession over this past year. We are confident that, although tired, you are well positioned to continue to give that, time and again, for the remainder of your career. Thank you, from the bottom of our hearts, for the work you do to make this world a better place.

Specific Skills

This section includes skills selected by you and the NS and added to the yearly planning guide/roadmap for Months 4-11. The NS should also select skills from this section to add into their trainees' roadmaps and use throughout the supervisory relationship. The skills included in this section do not represent an exhaustive list of the skills necessary to be a successful independent supervisor. Instead, we selected eleven specific skills that we consider foundational for a NS, and for supervisees and trainees who will soon become supervisors. These are skills that go above and beyond the BACB® Task List and the content included in the Getting Ready and the Early Months sections. These skills are critical to success, career longevity, and developing more advanced skills. The eleven skills are listed in alphabetical order and are as follows:

1. **Compassionate Care and Therapeutic Relationships**
2. **Enhancing Learning: Self-Monitoring, Describing, and Asking Meaningful Questions**
3. **Evaluating Effects of Supervision**
4. **Feedback and Difficult Conversations**
5. **Ongoing Monitoring and Performance Management**
6. **Organization and Time Management**
7. **Problem-Solving and Decision Making**
8. **Public Speaking and Professional Presentations**
9. **Scope of Competence**
10. **Self-Care**
11. **Teaching BST and Training Strategies**

Each section includes information that will be most relevant to developing the NS's skills and information that applies to developing the related skills of their supervisees and trainees. You and the NS should use the information from the skills assessments, as well as naturally arising needs, to select the most relevant skills from this section to include in your NS's roadmap for Month 4 through Month 11. However, we recognize the complexities of supervisory practice, and acknowledge that extra time may be spent working on one skill to mastery. Therefore, we include strategies and resources that the NS can use should they need to address some of their skill development after the relationship with you has ended.

Each specific skill includes the following sections:

1. a brief description of the skill(s),
2. a brief description of why the skill(s) is(are) important,
3. strategies for how to assess the skill(s),
4. suggestions for how to teach the skill(s), and
5. additional resources.

In the assessment section, specific strategies for assessing the skill are described and a table is provided with indicators for you and for your NSs to assist in evaluating if the skill is not yet acquired or is developing. Knowing where an individual is along the scope of skill development can help best identify teaching strategies and opportunities for shaping the skill. The teaching section discusses strategies for developing the relevant skill and includes a table with several possible reflective practices and actions. The strategies can be used collaboratively with you and the NS to build their skills. Work with the NS to set goals, track progress, and discuss how things are going in your monthly meetings. Review the agenda that the NS prepares to ensure they allot an appropriate amount of time on the agenda to discuss topics based on their need. They may ask you for the opportunity to role-play or practice some skills or activities. Check in with the NS regularly to discuss their use of the topics and strategies with their supervisees or trainees. Finally, you can use the reflective strategies and actions to continue to build your own skills as relevant.

Compassionate Care and Therapeutic Relationships

What These Are

Taylor et al. (2019) described compassionate care as providing services with an emphasis on empathy, compassion, and collaboration. Empathy involves both perceiving the feelings of others and understanding those emotions based on your own prior experiences with similar emotions. Compassionate care involves acting based on your understanding of the other person's experience in an effort to support them and alleviate their suffering.

Compassionate care occurs in the context of a therapeutic relationship with the client and family. Therapeutic relationships are enhanced when behavior analysts practice skills in the domain of listening and collaboration, demonstrate empathy and compassion, and avoid various "negative" behaviors that could contribute to problems in the therapeutic relationship (Taylor et al., 2019). See Taylor et al. (2019) for a full list of these skills, behaviors to avoid, and a proposed curriculum of skills to teach.

Why They Are Important

Taylor et al. (2019) made the case that therapeutic relationship skills (e.g., empathy, compassion, rapport building) are a critical part of the repertoire of a successful BCBA because of the potential positive impact on family satisfaction, adherence to treatment, and improved clinical outcomes. Taylor et al. (2019) further hypothesized that failure to engage in critical relationship skills may negatively impact treatment, including parental nonsupport of treatment recommendations, requests for reassignment to a different clinician, or termination of behavior-analytic services altogether. Use of these therapeutic relationship skills to create effective working relationships with clients and families can also directly influence practitioners themselves. LeBlanc, Sellers et al. (2020) describe that lack of these skills can lead to conflict-laden relationships with families which can erode professional experiences and lead to burnout for behavior analysts. Unfortunately, most behavior analysts are not trained in these skills as a part of their graduate training (LeBlanc et al., 2019). Whereas those articles were specific to the importance of compassionate care in the context of the therapeutic relationship between a clinician and a caregiver or client, it makes sense that many of the considerations and skills are also relevant to the supervisory relationship. In fact, LeBlanc, Sellers et al. (2020) describe these skills as a pivotal professional repertoire that should be explicitly taught in supervision.

Assessing These Skills

A supervisor could use a variety of strategies for assessing these skills. First, the supervisor could ask a supervisee or trainee to self-assess their use of specific strategies to establish and nurture a healthy therapeutic relationship with caregivers, supervisees, and trainees. LeBlanc, Sellers et al. (2020) provide a checklist for this purpose in Chapter 8. Second, these skills could be assessed and taught during role-plays of interactions with parents, supervisees, or trainees. The fifth column of

Table 5 in Taylor et al. (2019) provides a list of suggested measures that could be used during performance assessments. Third, these skills can be assessed by observing interactions with clients and families or supervisees and trainees to identify the presence or absence of component skills and by seeking feedback about those skills from clients, families, supervisees, and trainees via surveys. The basic skill indicators are described here.

Skill Level	New BCBA	Supervisees/Trainees
Not yet acquired	✓ Never or infrequently makes reflective statements during active listening ✓ Never or infrequently detects when a caregiver, client, supervisee, or trainee is becoming distressed ✓ Always or frequently pushes their own agenda or does not acknowledge the ideas, priorities or concerns of client, caregiver, supervisee, or trainee ✓ Unable to fluently describe what it might feel like to experience the daily concerns of the client, caregivers, supervisee, or trainee (i.e., perspective taking) ✓ Infrequently or never alters interactions in response to indicators that the other person is upset, agitated, or withdrawing ✓ Is not able to tolerate the discomfort that occurs when a caregiver, client, supervisee, or trainee engages in emotional responding (e.g., crying, expressing sadness)	✓ Same
Developing	✓ Makes some reflective statements during active listening ✓ Detects at least some instances of distress even if they are not the earliest indicators ✓ Frequently acknowledges the ideas, priorities and concerns of the caregiver, client, supervisee, or trainee and collaboratively designs programming based on these ✓ Able to engage in perspective-taking with respect to the experience of others (e.g., caring for a child with special needs, trying new and difficult skills) ✓ Demonstrates some responsiveness to indicators that the other person is upset, agitated, or withdrawing (e.g., sitting quietly to actively listen and responding empathetically when a caregiver, supervisee, or trainee is distressed or crying)	✓ Same

Teaching These Skills

A supervisor could use a variety of strategies to teach these skills. First, the supervisor could engage in an array of perspective-taking exercises with the supervisee or trainee. The supervisor could present a description of someone's circumstances along with a partial list of values (e.g., wanting to be a good parent and protect their child), concerns (e.g., Will my child ever be able to live independently?), and priorities (e.g., teach them to talk) that the parent/caregiver/guardian might have. They can then ask the supervisee or trainee to describe what it might feel like to live in these circumstances, providing descriptions if the supervisee cannot do so. The supervisor can also ask the supervisee or trainee to generate additional values, worries, priorities, or biases that the person in those circumstances might have. Second, the supervisor could ask a supervisee or trainee to practice several skills in front of a mirror so that they have immediate visual feedback on facial expressions and whether those expressions are concordant with their statements (e.g., "I care about collaboratively selecting meaningful goals for services" accompanied by an earnest and pleasant expression). The supervisee or trainee could also score their own behavior from a video of their performance during role-plays or live interactions with clients. Additional instructional strategies are described in column 4 of Table 5 in Taylor et al. (2019).

Use the reflection activities in the table below to help the NS or their trainees or to support your own skills in developing and maintaining therapeutic relationships.

Reflection	Action
✓ Think about the benefits of asking clients, supervisees, and trainees about their priorities and how those can be integrated into services.	✓ Review the relevant standards (2.09, 2.14, and 3.14) from the Ethics Code for Behavior Analysts (BACB, 2020).
✓ Use the self-assessments in LeBlanc, Sellers et al. to reflect on your use of therapeutic relationship skills with clients, caregivers, supervisees, and trainees.	✓ Make a list of phrases that can convey caring and empathy in interactions with clients, caregivers, supervisees, and trainees.
✓ Think about what principles of behavior analysis are involved in building a strong relationship with a client, caregiver, supervisee, and trainee.	✓ Identify strategies you could use to repair a therapeutic relationship that is currently not going well.
✓ Think about how one's own covert behavior (e.g., dreading a conversation with someone, feeling relieved when someone stops pushing to convey their priorities) can lead to destructive overt behavior (e.g., cutting someone off, pushing your own agenda, canceling meetings and sessions).	✓ Practice an upcoming conversation with a client, caregiver, supervisee, or trainee in which you might need to apologize, reestablish trust or motivation for services, or set appropriate boundaries.
	✓ Identify a mentor, supervisor, or trusted colleague who excels at these skills and approach them for guidance.

Resources

1. Fiske, K. E. (2017). *Autism and the family: Understanding and supporting parents and siblings.* Norton.

2. LeBlanc, L. A., Sellers, T. P., & Ala'i, S. (2020). *Building and sustaining meaningful and effective relationships as a supervisor and mentor.* Sloan Publishing.

3. LeBlanc, L. A., Taylor, B. A., & Marchese N. V. (2019). The training experiences of behavior analysts: Compassionate care and therapeutic relationships with caregivers. *Behavior Analysis in Practice, 13,* 387–393. https://doi.org/10.1007/s40617-019-00368-z

4. Stewart, John (Ed.) (1999). *Bridges not walls: A book about interpersonal communication.* 7th Ed. McGraw-Hill.

5. Stone, D., Patton, B. & Heen, S. (1999). *Difficult conversations: How to discuss what matters most.* Penguin Books.

6. Taylor, B. A., LeBlanc, L. A., & Nosik, M.R. (2019). Compassionate care in behavior analytic treatment: Can outcomes be enhanced by attending to relationships with caregivers? *Behavior Analysis in Practice, 12,* 654–666. https://org/10.1007/s40617-018-0089-3

7. Tulgan, B. (2015). *Bridging the soft skills gap: How to teach the missing basics to today's young talent.* Jossey-Bass.

Enhancing Learning: Self-Monitoring, Describing, and Asking Meaningful Questions

What These Are

You can teach your supervisees and trainees at least three active learning skills that can enhance continued learning: self-monitoring, self-narrating, and asking meaningful questions. Active learning, as opposed to passive observing and listening, can enhance learning throughout supervision. *Self-monitoring* refers to carefully attending to your own behavior, including actions, facial expressions, thoughts and feelings, and stimuli correlated with those behaviors (e.g., others' facial expressions, body language, and vocal responses) (LeBlanc, Sellers et al., 2020). Those responses can then be evaluated against a criterion to determine whether the behavior needs to change (Bandura, 1997). They can also be examined to find the functional determinants of your own performance. *Self-narrating* refers to carefully and precisely 1) describing your own actions while doing them or immediately afterward, 2) indicating specific aspects of your performance that were or were not satisfactory and why, and 3) indicating skills that need improvement and why (LeBlanc, Sellers et al., 2020). *Asking meaningful questions* refers to formulating your thoughts before communicating to a supervisor, manager, or colleague so that questions specify the information that is needed and illustrate the actions you have already taken or thought through. It takes thoughtful preparation to ask a meaningful question and supervision presents the perfect opportunity to establish this skill.

Why They Are Important

When we develop robust repertoires for active learning, we increase the chances that we will be able to continue to learn and evolve our skills once we operate independently (i.e., without supervision). These skills help a person evaluate their own performance as well as the variables that are influencing their performance at any given time. Once we can simultaneously behave and evaluate our own behavior, we can rapidly correct our own behavior and learn from our mistakes more quickly and effectively. We are also likely to have a fuller understanding of why we should make certain clinical choices rather than simply following rules or previously observed examples. These skills also allow a person to make the most out of the time that they spend in continuing education or with a supervisor or consultant. Finally, these skills enhance our ability to evaluate our own scope of competence and to potentially expand that scope of competence through observations and interactions with experts.

Assessing These Skills

Each of these skills can be assessed in the context of supervised or independent practice. The best way to assess self-monitoring skills is to directly compare data collected on one's own behavior to data collected by an independent observer. When using self-monitoring as a therapeutic intervention, the first step is always to teach and reinforce accurate data collection. The same approach can be taken with supervisees and trainees. One of the most direct ways to assess a person's skills in performing and narrating their actions is to have them engage in a well-learned skill and collect data on 1) the speed of the skill compared to when they are not self-narrating, 2) the accuracy of the skill compared to when they are not self-narrating, and 3) the amount of detail in the narrative description. Additionally, you can ask them the questions about their performance that illustrate whether they are able to identify decision points and desired outcomes. Finally, questions that are posed in supervision can be scored with respect to the extent to which they match the definition of a meaningful question and guide the supervisor's actions rather than taking the form of a statement (e.g., "I don't understand this.") or simple request for help (e.g., "Can you help me find a resource?").

Skill Level	New BCBA	Supervisees/Trainees
Not yet acquired	✓ Unable to accurately score their own performance in a task ✓ Infrequently or never performs and narrates actions without disruption to performance ✓ Unable to describe the risks of not evaluating whether a perceived expert is actually an expert ✓ Infrequently or never accurately describes a desired outcome for an observed sequence ✓ Infrequently or never accurately identifies decision points in an observed performance ✓ Information is usually sought by making statements (e.g., "I don't understand") rather than asking meaningful questions.	✓ Unable to accurately score their own performance in a task ✓ Infrequently or never accurately describes how they would or did complete a task ✓ Infrequently or never accurately identifies decision points in an observed performance ✓ Frequently or always requires someone else to point out when their performance is not accurate or sufficient ✓ Information is usually sought by making statements (e.g., "I don't understand") rather than asking meaningful questions.

Skill Level	New BCBA	Supervisees/Trainees
Developing	✓ Frequently scores their own performance on a task with accuracy as they complete the task ✓ Frequently describes an observed sequence of events with accuracy ✓ Frequently determines whether the observed sequence resulted in the desired outcome ✓ Frequently describes why an observed response occurred rather than a different response ✓ Frequently identifies decision points that occurred during the observed performance and why each decision was made ✓ Frequently performs a task at normal speed while narrating actions ✓ Frequently asks meaningful questions focused on gaining information or evaluating own performance	✓ Able to accurately score their own performance in a task as they complete the task ✓ Frequently describes how they would or did complete a task with accuracy ✓ Frequently identifies decision points in an observed performance with accuracy ✓ Frequently identifies when their performance is not accurate or sufficient ✓ Frequently seeks information by asking meaningful questions focused on gaining information or evaluating own performance

Teaching These Skills

A supervisor can teach these skills by modeling each one. For example, when a supervisor performs a task and subsequently *debriefs* (i.e., describes what they did, why they did it, whether they encountered any decision points and why they made the decision that they did), they are modeling delayed narration of their task. They can also model simultaneous self-narration if the audible narration will not affect client services. Prior to or after modeling, the supervisor can explain why they narrate their actions and how it can be helpful to do so in one's professional activities.

A supervisor can also take a structured didactic approach to teaching these skills. For example, a supervisor could describe their three criteria for a meaningful question and provide examples and non-examples. They could subsequently provide feedback on the questions that are brought to supervision with an opportunity to restate any questions that don't meet the criteria. For self-monitoring and self-narrating, the supervisor could assign Chapter 6 of LeBlanc, Sellers et al., (2020) along with self-monitoring and self-narrating tasks. The supervisor can have the supervisee select a skill they can already do well and have them narrate their actions (LeBlanc, Sellers et al., 2020). Selecting an intact skill will minimize the chances that narrating disrupts the performance, but initial attempts at self-narration may still slow performance or create errors, so select the skill wisely. If this happens, the person can practice narration while they are viewing video footage of their prior performance.

If the practice occurs during live performance, the supervisor can have the supervisee perform the skill at a slightly slower-than-typical pace and simultaneously narrate the steps in the response as they are performed

(LeBlanc, Sellers et al., 2020). Once the supervisee can vocally narrate the discrete responses or behavior, the supervisor can teach the supervisee to add a narration of their private events (i.e., "Describe what you are doing and what thoughts you are having about your performance"). Next, the supervisor can have the supervisee narrate any decision points that occur and why they made the decisions that they did.

Reflection	Action
✓ Think about the role of careful attending in observational learning. ✓ Think about the role of curiosity in asking meaningful questions. ✓ Think about the processes involved in engaging in an action and simultaneously narrating that action overtly or covertly. ✓ Think about the consequences of failing to notice decision points in your applied practice. ✓ Identify a time when you observed an expert's performance but failed to fully understand the behavior you were observing and why it was occurring.	✓ Review the relevant standards (5.10) from the Ethics Code for Behavior Analysts (BACB, 2020). ✓ Identify an expert and a popular non-expert in the same area. Describe the differences in their behavior, statements, and recommendations. ✓ Practice performing and narrating actions and choices until fluent. ✓ Write meaningful questions prior to your supervision sessions and include them in your agenda. ✓ Observe an expert and ask curious and meaningful questions about their actions and choice during the performance.

Resources

1. LeBlanc, L. A., Sellers, T. P., & Ala'i, S. (2020). *Building and sustaining meaningful and effective relationships as a supervisor and mentor*. Sloan Publishing.

Evaluating Effects of Supervision

What This Is

Evaluating the effects of one's supervisory practices involves collecting and evaluating data to determine if those practices are producing the desired outcomes (LeBlanc, Sellers et al., 2020; Sellers, Valentino et al., 2020; Turner et al. 2016). Evaluations should take place for each trainee throughout the supervisory relationship. Data should be considered form a variety of sources such as the trainee's performance and feedback, client performance, and caregiver and peer feedback. Supervisors should also evaluate the outcomes across multiple supervisory relationships to ensure that their practices are consistently effective over time and for a variety of trainees. For more guidance on how and what to evaluate, see recommendations in Chapter 10 of LeBlanc, Sellers et al. (2020) and the articles by Sellers, Valentino et al. (2020) and Turner et al. (2016).

Why This Is Important

Certified behavior analysts are required to take an active role in continually assessing the outcomes of their supervisory practices and strengthening related repertoires through professional learning opportunities. Specifically, standard 4.02 Supervisory Competence (BACB, 2020), states: "Behavior analysts supervise and train others only within their identified scope of competence. They provide supervision only after obtaining knowledge and skills in effective supervisory practices, and they continually evaluate and improve their supervisory repertoires through professional development" (p. 15). The function of this standard is to hold supervisors accountable for demonstrating that they and their trainees are achieving the targeted outcomes. This is critical for many reasons, including being able to replicate positive effects, identify and respond to any deficiencies to protect clients and trainees, and increase the likelihood that trainees will be successful in their future clinical and supervisory endeavors.

Assessing This Skill

One of the most direct ways to assess a supervisor's skills in this area is to simply ask them how they are evaluating the outcomes of their supervisory practices. A competent supervisor will outline the different sources of data and frequency with which they engage in such evaluation. If a full and well-structured response is not immediately produced, that is a good indicator that the supervisor needs to develop their skills in this area. A more in-depth assessment includes reviewing the sources of the supervisor's evaluation. For example, it will be important to review any formal feedback forms that the individual is using, as well as evidence that the feedback is regularly sought, reviewed, and responded to in a meaningful way. Other resources to review the supervisor include documentation that they have regularly scheduled self-evaluations in their calendar and that they are actively collecting, reviewing, and responding to data from a variety of sources.

Use the indicators below to identify where a new BCBA's or supervisee's/trainee's skills fall. For supervisees (e.g., RBTs, BCaBAs) this will only be relevant if they provide supervision to others, and expectations should be adjusted for their skill level. For trainees, this will likely be relevant toward the end of the fieldwork experience, as they take on more responsibilities and move closer to becoming an independent clinician and supervisor. For both supervisees and trainees, their evaluation of their supervisory practices should always be facilitated and overseen by a supervisor.

Skill Level	New BCBA	Supervisees/Trainees
Not yet acquired	✓ Infrequently or never describes the importance of evaluating the outcomes of one's supervisory practices ✓ Infrequently or never describes the risks of not evaluating the outcomes of one's supervisory practices ✓ Infrequently or never describes a variety of data sources ✓ Infrequently or never solicits feedback and guidance about their supervisory practices ✓ Infrequently or never receives feedback in an appropriate manner (e.g., gets defensive, shuts down) ✓ Infrequently or never implements changes based on feedback and data indicating that their supervisory practices are ineffective	✓ Same
Developing	✓ Able to provide some indicators of the importance of evaluating one's supervisory practices ✓ Able to describe some of the risks of not evaluating the outcomes of one's supervisory practices ✓ Able to describe some data sources ✓ Can describe why it is important to respond to feedback and data indicating that their supervisory practices are ineffective ✓ Frequently solicits feedback and guidance about their supervisory practices ✓ Frequently receives feedback in an appropriate manner (e.g., actively listens, makes statements of appreciation and accountability) ✓ Frequently implements changes based on feedback and data that indicate their supervisory practices are ineffective	✓ Same

Teaching This Skill

Evaluating the effects of one's supervisory practices relies on a variety of component skills (e.g., data collection, soliciting feedback, evaluating data, having crucial conversations, self-management); therefore, it can be helpful to teach these component skills individually early on so that they can then be leveraged together to support this evaluation. Mentors and supervisors can facilitate the growth of these skills in new BCBAs and trainees by clearly describing the process and why it is important. Modeling and guided practice are likely to be effective strategies for teaching and strengthening the repertoires needed to carry out an evaluation of one's supervisory practices. This can be done by showing the new BCBA or trainee the types of data to collect, examples of data collection and feedback forms, how to create their own capture systems, and by walking them through the process of reviewing and responding to the data collected. It may also be critical to highlight other useful prompts like recurring calendar reminders and related tasks on their curricular roadmaps for their supervisees and trainees.

Use the reflection activities together with your NS or by yourself to support your skills in evaluating the effects of your supervision.

Reflection	Action
✓ Think about the benefits of continually evaluating the effects of one's supervisory practices and the risks of failing to do so.	✓ Review the relevant standards (1.05, 1.06, and 4.02) from the Ethics Code for Behavior Analysts (BACB, 2020).
✓ Think about which dimensions of behavior analysis are related to engaging in this evaluation.	✓ Make a list of the sources of data that should be evaluated.
✓ Think about the processes involved in programming for clients and how those same practices can be leveraged to evaluate the outcomes of supervisory practices.	✓ Identify how frequently the different sources of data should be collected and evaluated. (Note that the schedule should be more frequently for newer supervisors and at the outset of any relationship.)
✓ Think about how one's own covert behavior (e.g., dreading or looking forward to supervision meetings, feeling relieved or disappointed when meetings are cancelled) and overt behavior (e.g., disengaged or engaged in meetings, frequently canceling meetings) can be used to support this evaluation.	✓ Find or create needed forms.
	✓ Practice conversations for soliciting feedback from supervisors, supervisees, caregivers, peers, etc.
✓ Think about how soliciting, receiving, implementing, and providing feedback can positively or negatively impact the supervisory relationship.	✓ Identify a mentor, supervisor, or trusted colleague with more supervisory experience with whom you can review and evaluate the data collected.

Resources

1. Behavior Analyst Certification Board. (2020). *Ethics code for behavior analysts.* Littleton, CO: Author.

2. LeBlanc, L. A., Sellers, T. P., & Ala'i, S. (2020). *Building and sustaining meaningful and effective relationships as a supervisor and mentor.* Sloan Publishing.

3. Sellers, T. P., Valentino, A. L., & LeBlanc, L. A. (2016). Recommended practices for individual supervision of aspiring behavior analysts. *Behavior Analysis in Practice*, 9(4), 274-286.

4. Turner, L. B., Fischer, A. J., & Luiselli, J. K. (2016). Towards a competency-based, ethical, and socially valid approach to the supervision of applied behavior analytic trainees. *Behavior Analysis in Practice*, 9(4), 287-298.

Feedback and Difficult Conversations

What These Are

Feedback is not only one of the most frequently used interventions to impact performance in human-service settings (Gravina et al., 2018), it has been demonstrated to be a critical component of BST (Ward-Horner & Sturmey, 2012). For our purposes, feedback is information given to a trainee or supervisee about their past performance that functions to inform their future performance. That is, feedback can be specific praise that identifies actions the trainee did well that results in them performing the skill in that same manner in the future. Feedback can also be specific information identifying problematic aspects of their performance and actions they should take in the future to improve. LeBlanc, Sellers et al. (2020) provide descriptions of the main sub-types of feedback (e.g., adequacy, diagnostic, corrective, supportive) in Chapter 5 of their book.

In practice, several considerations relate to feedback. One set of considerations focuses the parameters of feedback (e.g., timing, magnitude, order, ratio of positive to corrective) for an individual (Chapters 2 and 5 in LeBlanc, Sellers et al, 2020). The parameters of feedback can, and should, be individualized for the recipient and context. The other set of considerations has to do with the larger classes of feedback skills needed to be a successful clinician and supervisor—soliciting, receiving, implementing, and giving feedback. Each of those components rely on slightly different but interrelated skills. For example, giving feedback requires skills related to perspective taking, in-the-moment discrimination, decision making, and interpersonal communication, to name a few. Implementing feedback, on the other hand, requires not only discrimination skills, but also self-reflection, evaluation, and management skills. Supervisors must also document feedback provided and effectively teach the components related to feedback to their trainees and supervisees.

In addition to general feedback skills, it is inevitable that BCBAs will have to have difficult conversations with supervisees, trainees, caregivers, colleagues, and other professionals. In the book *Crucial Conversations*, the authors define *crucial* (aka difficult) conversations as those that focus on something important or critical, involve differences of opinions, and wherein emotions run high (Grenny et al. 2022). Chapter 9 in the book by LeBlanc, Sellers et al. (2020) covers interpersonal- and therapeutic-relations skills and provides many helpful strategies for increasing the quality of communication skills, particularly related to difficult topics. Some examples of crucial conversations for BCBAs include conversations when providing critical corrective feedback, during a discussion addressing that feedback has not been implemented, when disagreeing about treatment options.

Why They Are Important

Effective repertoires related to feedback are critical to successfully teaching and shaping supervisee and trainee performance. Providing and teaching high-quality feedback to supervisees and trainees can

1. improve their clinical performance,
2. build their repertoires to be successful supervisors,
3. increase positive outcomes for clients, and
4. create and maintain a positive supervisory relationship.

Alternatively, providing low-quality feedback, or avoiding it all together, can result in the development of defective or harmful clinical and supervisory repertoires for the supervisee or trainee, harm to clients, and damage to the supervisory relationship. Therefore, it is critical the supervisors develop well-rounded repertoires for giving, soliciting, receiving, implementing, and documenting feedback, as well as expressly teaching all the components to their trainees.

Difficult or crucial conversations are important because many of us have not been explicitly taught the skills necessarily to navigate them successfully. Many of us tend to avoid them, which can lead to a worsening of the problem and even direct risks of harm. Others of us may address them, but not in a skilled and purposeful manner. For examples, we may be so indirect that the listener cannot discriminate that we are providing feedback about their performance. Alternatively, we may be so direct that we create such an aversive experience that prevents the listener from being able to receive the critical information about their performance. In either of these extremes, it is unlikely that the individual's performance will change, and we may damage the supervisory relationship.

Assessing These Skills

Feedback and difficult conversation skills can be assessed through discussion, case-examples, role-play, and observation. For example, these skills could be tested by role-playing or watching video examples of feedback delivery and asking the individual to score or describe

1. what went well and why,
2. what did not go well and why, and
3. what should be done to correct the issue.

Assessments should include multiple exemplars across contexts and feedback components. For example, it is likely insufficient to only assess an individual's ability to give feedback and not assess their ability to solicit, receive, implement, and document feedback. Similarly, evaluating an individual's ability to provide high-quality feedback to an RBT while failing to evaluate their ability in relation to caregivers, colleagues, and other professionals probably results in an incomplete picture of their skills.

Skill Level	New BCBA	Supervisees/Trainees
Not yet acquired	✓ Unable to describe 　○ the function of feedback 　○ the components of high-quality feedback 　○ the risks of low-quality of feedback or failure to provide feedback 　○ strategies for soliciting feedback 　○ strategies for implementing feedback 　○ strategies for navigating difficult conversations ✓ Unable to effectively 　○ role-play delivering, receiving, or teaching feedback 　○ teach others skills related to feedback ✓ Consistent difficulty with or avoidance of giving, soliciting, receiving, implementing, and documenting feedback or having difficult conversations	✓ Difficulty receiving and implementing feedback ✓ Difficulty with, or absence of giving feedback to supervisor ✓ Difficulty with, or absence of soliciting feedback from supervisor
Developing	✓ Able to describe some components of high-quality feedback and difficult conversations (listed above) ✓ Able to engage in role-play and discussions with some success ✓ Frequently gives, solicits, receives, implements, and documents feedback and has some difficult conversations with some success	✓ Some success receiving and implementing feedback ✓ Some success with, or attempts to give feedback to supervisor ✓ Some success with, or attempts to solicit feedback from supervisor

Teaching These Skills

These skills should be expressly taught, using BST. Discussions should include multiple exemplars, the benefits related to high-quality feedback and engaging in difficult conversations, as well as the risks of low-quality feedback, no feedback, and avoiding difficult conversations. A supervisor could use written descriptions or movie clips depicting things like feedback solicitation, reception, delivery, or a difficult conversation and role-plays to teach these skills. After a model or role-play, an individual should engage in the same three steps described in the assessment section. In instances where the feedback delivery or difficult conversations needed to be corrected, the individual could subsequently role-play a corrected version and then debrief about the improvements and if they were successful. Individuals can be provided with samples of lists of the critical components of feedback delivery and reception; scripts for giving and soliciting feedback; scripts for navigating difficult conversations; feedback solicitation and documentation forms; and checklists for teaching each of these skills to practice and use. See the resources list for valuable articles and books to facilitate teaching skills related to feedback delivery and navigating difficult conversations. Many helpful resources are available in the LeBlanc, Sellers et al. (2020) book, including the following:

- Chapter 2 Activity: Exploring Collaboration Topics, p. 24
- Chapter 2 Appendix: How to Talk About Feedback, p. 26
- Chapter 5 Table with examples of how to convert feedback statements, p. 87
- Chapter 5 Appendix C: Script for Explaining Feedback and Responding to Feedback, p. 94
- Chapter 11 Case Example 2 A Supervisor's Harsh Feedback, p. 223

Use the reflection activities together with your NS or by yourself to support development of skills in accepting and delivering feedback and handling difficult conversations.

Reflection	Action
✓ Think about your past experiences giving and receiving feedback or having difficult conversations and what the outcomes were. ✓ Think about how your supervisees and trainees (and others) respond to your feedback or difficult conversations. ✓ Think about past instances when you avoided providing feedback to, or having difficult conversations with a supervisor, supervisee, trainee, or other individual: 　○ Why do you think you avoided it? 　○ What was the outcome? ✓ Think about a time when you are pretty sure that someone did not provide you with feedback or have a difficult conversation with you that could have helped you improved: 　○ Why do you think they avoided it? 　○ What was the outcome?	✓ Write out some of the statements you typically use to give different types of feedback or navigate difficult conversations and then edit them for improvement (e.g., more compassionate, objective, specific). ✓ Write out some common specific feedback and difficult conversation scenarios to practice with yourself and use in your supervision. ✓ Start collecting video examples of high-quality and low-quality feedback and difficult conversations from movies and shows to use in your supervision. ✓ Develop a list of critical components for high-quality feedback and difficult conversations to use in your supervision for scoring yourself and for teaching trainees. ✓ Review your forms for soliciting feedback and edit for improvement. ✓ Access the articles and books in the resource list and calendar time to review each, discuss with colleagues, and create follow-up tasks.

Resources

1. Ehrlich, R. J., Nosik, M. R., Carr, J. E., & Wine, B. (2020). Teaching employees how to receive feedback: A preliminary investigation. *Journal of Organizational Behavior Management, 40*(1-2), 19-29.

2. Gravina, N., Villacorta, J., Albert, K., Clark, R., Curry, S., & Wilder, D. (2018). A literature review of organizational behavior management interventions in human service settings from 1990 to 2016. *Journal of Organizational Behavior Management, 38*(23), 191–224. doi:10.1080/01608061.2018.1454872

3. Grenny, J., Patterson, K., McMillan, R., Switzler, A., & Gregory, E. (2022). *Crucial conversations: Tools for talking when stakes are high* (3rd ed.). McGraw Hill.

4. Kazemi, E., Rice, B., & Adzhyan, P. (2018). *Fieldwork and supervision for behavior analysts: A handbook*. Springer Publishing Company.

5. LeBlanc, L. A., Sellers, T. P., & Ala'i, S. (2020). *Building and sustaining meaningful and effective relationships as a supervisor and mentor*. Sloan Publishing.

6. Scott, K. (2019). *Radical candor: Be a kick-ass boss without losing your humanity* (fully revised & updated ed.). St. Martin's Press.

7. Sellers, T. P., LeBlanc, L. A., & Valentino, A. L. (2016). Recommendations for detecting and addressing barriers to successful supervision. *Behavior Analysis in Practice, 9*(4), 309-319.

8. Sellers, T. P., Valentino, A. L., & LeBlanc, L. A. (2016). Recommended practices for individual supervision of aspiring behavior analysts. *Behavior Analysis in Practice, 9*(4), 274-286.

9. Stone, D., Patton, B., & Heen, S. (2010). *Difficult conversations: How to discuss what matters most* (10th anniversary ed.). Penguin Books.

10. Turner, L. B., Fischer, A. J., & Luiselli, J. K. (2016). Towards a competency-based, ethical, and socially valid approach to the supervision of applied behavior analytic trainees. *Behavior Analysis in Practice, 9*(4), 287-298.

11. Walker, S., & Sellers, T. (2021). Teaching appropriate feedback reception skills using computer-based instruction: A systematic replication. *Journal of Organizational Behavior Management, 41*(3), 236-254.

12. Ward-Horner, J., & Sturmey, P. (2012). Component analysis of behavior skills training in functional analysis. *Behavioral Interventions, 27*(2), 75–92.

Ongoing Monitoring and Performance Management

What These Are

Ongoing monitoring refers to the continual review and evaluation of services delivered to someone, whether that is a client, a supervisee, or a trainee. Typically, ongoing monitoring of clinical programing involves collecting and reviewing data on the acquisition and reductive programming in place to identify the degree to which the desired outcomes are being achieved, and to make timely decisions related to those data. For example, a client who is making consistent and rapid progress will require introducing new targets and programs and a client who is not demonstrating maintenance of previously mastered skills may require adjustments to instructional strategies and mastery criteria. When we talk about ongoing monitoring and performance management of supervisees and trainees, we are generally referring to observing the performance of skills the supervisee or trainee is learning or has learned, collecting and evaluating data, and providing any needed coaching. As with clients, consistent review of their performance allows a supervisor to 1) ensure they are implementing skills and carrying out tasks accurately; 2) assess progress, maintenance, and generalization; and 3) identify needs, make decisions, and implement adjustments in a timely manner (Parsons et al. 2012). If any performance needs are detected, supervisors can immediately provide feedback, coaching, or additional training. If the supervisor is unsuccessful in addressing the performance need, they can implement a functional assessment, such as the Performance Diagnostic Checklist – Human Services (PDC-HS; Carr et al., 2013) of the contextual barriers and develop a well-matched performance-improvement plan for the supervisee or trainee.

Why They Are Important

Failing to engage in ongoing monitoring of clients, supervisees, and trainees, can negatively impact progress, invite risks of harm, and result in wasted time and resources (LeBlanc, Sellers et al., 2020). For supervisees and trainees, failing to implement ongoing monitoring and performance management of their acquisition can also result in them feeling unsupported, questioning their abilities, or assuming that they are doing well when that might not be the case. If performance issues exist, particularly those that are resistant to initial feedback, failing to implement performance management can worsen the issue and invite risk of harm to clients and others. Taking a structured approach to performance management that includes collecting data, goal setting, and planning structured supports allows the supervisor to carefully monitor the effects of the plan and make systematic adjustments as needed.

Assessing These Skills

New BCBAs and more advanced trainees should be engaging in ongoing monitoring and performance management of clients, supervisees, and trainees. Having a discussion with the individual wherein you ask specific questions can be helpful in evaluating their level of knowledge and skill related to ongoing monitoring. Some questions include the following: What is ongoing monitoring or performance management? Why is it important to engage in ongoing monitoring or performance management? What are some ways to engage in ongoing monitoring of clients, supervisees, and trainees and performance management of supervisees and trainees? These skills can be assessed by asking to see the schedule for ongoing monitoring and the practices used (e.g., reviewing data, observing, collecting satisfaction feedback). It may be the case that an individual engages in ongoing monitoring of clients but *not* of their supervisees or trainees, which is an indication of a failure to generalize the skill. Another method of assessment is to provide case scenarios and ask the individual to identify on what schedule they would engage in ongoing monitoring or performance management, how they would do so, and the behaviors they would look for in their monitoring, and the actions they would take to address any issues.

When using case scenarios to assess skills related to performance management, the focus should be on assessing if they can clearly identify the performance issue, evaluate the contributing environmental barriers, and outline a performance-management plan to address this issue, or indicate that they would use a structured tool, such as the PDC-HS (Carr et al. 2013). See articles by Garza et al. (2018); Sellers, LeBlanc, et al. (2016); and Sellers, Valentino, et al. (2016) for considerations and resources to assist in assessing these skills.

Use the indicators listed below to assess skills related to ongoing monitoring and performance management.

Skill Level	New BCBA	Supervisees/Trainees
Not yet acquired	✓ Unable to describe ongoing monitoring and performance management and why they are important for clinical programming and supervising others ✓ Unable to describe strategies for ongoing monitoring for clinical programming and supervisees ✓ Unable to describe strategies for performance management of staff ✓ Infrequently or never identifies present or emerging clinical or performance issues in a timely manner or at all	✓ Unable to describe ongoing monitoring and why it is important for clinical programming ✓ Unable to describe strategies for ongoing monitoring of clinical programming ✓ Infrequently or never detects possible needs in clinical programming in a timely manner or at all ✓ Infrequently or never alerts supervisor of possible needs in clinical programming in a timely manner
Developing	✓ Able to provide some description of ongoing monitoring and performance management and why they are important for clinical programming and supervising others ✓ Able to describe and frequently implements some strategies for ongoing monitoring of clinical programming and supervisees ✓ Able to describe and frequently implements some strategies for performance management of staff	✓ Able to provide some description of ongoing monitoring and why it is important for clinical programming ✓ Able to describe and frequently implements some strategies for ongoing monitoring of clinical programming ✓ Frequently detects some possible needs in clinical programming in a timely manner ✓ Frequently alerts supervisor of possible needs in clinical programming in a timely manner

Teaching These Skills

BST can be used to teach the practice of ongoing monitoring and performance management, with heavy use of role-play and supported practice. In addition, BST should include multiple exemplars that represent the conditions likely to be present in the natural environment. For example, present the individual with a variety of learner and performer profiles and patterns. For clients, this might include learner profiles along a continuum of complexity (e.g., absence or presence of other health needs, severe problem behavior, communication needs, fine and gross motor needs, sensory deficits) and learner patterns (e.g., slow acquisition, fast acquisition, variable responding, failure to acquire certain types of programs, plateauing, failure to maintain or generalize skills). For supervisees and trainees, the case examples may include some of those same learning patterns and some different patterns of responding (e.g., argumentative, difficult or failure accepting and/or implementing feedback). Teach using a functional-assessment approach to persistent issues, such as how to implement the PDC-HS (Carr et al., 2013) and develop a matched plan to support the individual and improve their performance. Use case scenarios and practice completing the PDC-HS, draft matched plans, and discuss what they would monitor to evaluate if the plan was successful and what they would do if it was not. The articles in the resource list provide recommendations and guidance for addressing these skills.

The reflection and actions items below can be used in building skills related to ongoing monitoring and performance management.

Reflection	Action

✓ Reflect on why it is critical to engage in ongoing monitoring of clinical programming and supervision (e.g., risk, benefits).
 	
✓ Reflect on why it is critical to engage in performance management of supervisees and trainees.
 	
✓ Reflect on any past experiences where clinical issues or performance issues were not detected in a timely manner:
  ◦ What were the outcomes?
  ◦ How could the issue or need have been identified earlier?
 	
✓ Reflect on a time when performance issues were identified in a trainee or supervisee but were not systematically addressed:
  ◦ Did the issue improve or worsen?
  ◦ What were the negative impacts?
	✓ Create a schedule for clients, supervisees, and trainees for ongoing progress monitoring.
	
	✓ Create a form for conducting ongoing progress monitoring for clients, supervisees, and trainees.
	
	✓ Create a list of critical performance indicators for supervisees and trainees (e.g., timeliness, accuracy in data and billing records, confidentiality, safety, client respect and dignity) and begin to create performance monitoring and integrity forms.
	
	✓ Create a policy and resources (e.g., formal feedback documentation, performance-improvement plan templates) for addressing persistent performance issues.
	
	✓ Create scripts for discussing performance management of persistent performance issues.

Resources

1. Carr, J. E., Wilder, D. A., Majdalany, L., Mathisen, D., & Strain, L. A. (2013). An assessment-based solution to a human-service employee performance problem. *Behavior Analysis in Practice, 6,* 16–32.

2. Garza, K. L., McGee, H. M., Schenk, Y. A., & Wiskirchen, R. R. (2018). Some tools for carrying out a proposed process for supervising experience hours for aspiring Board-Certified Behavior Analysts®. *Behavior Analysis in Practice, 11,* 62–70.

3. LeBlanc, L. A., Sellers, T. P., & Ala'i, S. (2020). *Building and sustaining effective relationships as a supervisor and mentor.* Sloan Publishing.

4. Parsons, M. B., Rollyson, J. H., & Reid, D. H. (2012). Evidence-based staff training. *Behavior Analysis in Practice, 5,* 2–11. doi: 10.1007/BF03391819

5. Sellers, T. P., Valentino, A. L., & LeBlanc, L. A. (2016). Recommended practices for individual supervision of aspiring behavior analysts. *Behavior Analysis in Practice, 9,* 274–286. doi:10.1007/s40617-016-0110-7

Organization and Time Management

What These Are

Organizational skills refer to planning and prioritizing activities and projects, goal setting, and organizing materials so they are easy to find when needed. Managing emails, electronic calendars, and electronic file storage and sharing systems are critical skills for success in today's practice environment. *Time management* refers to planning the use of available time in line with priorities, personal goals and lifestyles, and professional demands (LeBlanc, Sellers et al., 2020). For example, a new BCBA must learn how to manage all the tasks associated with effectively managing their caseload (e.g., assessment, report writing, selecting goals, writing programs, analyzing data and modifying programs, providing supervision, meeting with parents) efficiently or many of these tasks may be neglected or pushed into non-work time (e.g., evenings, weekends). Managing meetings is a subskill in this area that becomes increasingly important as a trainee transitions into independent practice and supervising others. Leading meetings effectively requires advanced planning and creation of an agenda and management of time during the meeting to accomplish the tasks included on the agenda (LeBlanc & Nosik, 2019).

Why They Are Important

LeBlanc, Sellers et al. (2020) refers to these skills as *pivotal* as they set the upper limit of what a person can achieve with their other skill sets. These skills allow a person to achieve goals in the minimum time possible through planning and self-management. They are also critical for managing stress while remaining productive (Allen, 2015). These skills have been shown to be related to successful transition into the workforce in practice-related disciplines (Ervin, 2008).

Unfortunately, poor time management skills can result in increased stress and depression, procrastination, and difficulties in managing job duties. LeBlanc, Sleeper, et al. (2020) found that OTM skills (e.g., explicit use of strategies, efficiency and effectiveness of task completion, proportion of primary activities off task) were the best predictor of success or failure in caseload management skills for BCBAs. These skills were more predictive of success or failure than other variables that we might expect to matter (e.g., size of caseload, match between client needs and clinical skills, and funding constraints).

Assessing These Skills

LeBlanc, Sellers et al. (2020) Chapter 8, Appendix D provides an assessment of organization and time-management skills. This narrative assessment is a good place to start identifying skills to refine. Allen & Hall (2019) provide an *Assess Your Reality* tool in Chapter 2 of their *Getting Things Done Workbook*. This assessment is scored, and the summed score can be compared to score ranges that indicate your progress on recommended practices for organization and time management. Finally, LeBlanc & Nosik (2019) provide a checklist that can be used to guide meeting planning and management and to evaluate meetings that have already occurred. In addition to these more comprehensive assessments, the following indicators can be used to determine if there may be problems with these skills.

Skill Level	New BCBA	Supervisees/Trainees
Not yet acquired	✓ Does not have a system for scheduling time or does not stick to the schedule that they create ✓ Does not keep an actions list or write down ideas as soon as they occur ✓ Frequently or always slow to respond or does not respond to emails, texts, and phone messages ✓ Frequently or always late to meetings or has to leave in the middle of a task due to overlapping commitments ✓ Frequently commits to more things than they can actually do ✓ Infrequently or never creates agendas or manages meeting time to accomplish the items on the agenda	✓ Same
Developing	✓ Frequently manages time and tasks efficiently ✓ Frequently keeps track of all assigned tasks and new ideas ✓ Frequently seeks clarification about tasks ✓ Frequently breaks down complex tasks into a series of smaller, actionable steps ✓ Frequently estimates how long it will take to accomplish a task with accuracy ✓ Frequently accesses information using technology resources in an effective and timely manner ✓ Frequently manages meeting time well, according to LeBlanc & Nosik (2019) checklist	✓ Same

Teaching/Refining These Skills

Self-assessment of these skills often produces some degree of insight about problems that have not previously been recognized as such. This is important because interventions for these skills may not be successful if the person does not acknowledge that their skills are sub-par. After self-assessment, a supervisor can teach these skills using BST. A variety of print resource materials on organization and time management are available. One particularly easy one to use is *The Getting Things Done Workbook* (Allen & Hall 2019).

Reflection	Action
✓ Think about the relationship between stress and organization and time management.	✓ Make a list of your upcoming tasks.
✓ Think about recent tasks that were not completed or were not completed on time and the direct or indirect consequences.	✓ Identify a tool to use to capture your ideas as they come up.
✓ Think about the role of stimulus control in managing task lists and schedules.	✓ Develop and implement a system for triaging and archiving your emails.
✓ Assess your own stress level.	✓ Identify tasks that are often delayed and analyze why these tasks are not completed when they should be.
✓ Assess your strategies using the tools in Allen & Hall (2019).	✓ Identify a mentor, supervisor, or trusted colleague with exceptional organization and time-management skills and interview them about their strategies.

Resources

1. Allen, D. A., & Hall, B. (2019). *The getting things done workbook: 10 moves to stress-free productivity*. Platkus.

2. Learn higher. (n.d.). Time management. Retrieved from http://www.learnhigher.ac.uk/learning-at-university/time-management/

3. LeBlanc, L. A., Sellers, T. P., & Ala'i, S. (2020). *Building and sustaining meaningful and effective relationships as a supervisor and mentor*. Sloan Publishing.

4. LeBlanc, L. A., Sleeper, J. D., Mueller, J. R., Jenkins, S. R., & Harper-Briggs, A. M. (2020). Assessing barriers to effective caseload management by practicing behavior analysts. *Journal of Organizational Behavior Management, 39*(3–4), 317–336.

5. LeBlanc, L. A., & Nosik, M. R. (2019). Planning and leading effective meetings. *Behavior Analysis in Practice, 12*, 696–708.

6. Lencioni, P. (2004). *Death by meeting*. Jossey-Bass.

7. Mind Tools Content Team. (n.d.) *S.M.A.R.T. goals: How to make your goals achievable*. Mind tools. https://www.mindtools/smart-goals.htm

8. Moronz-Alpert, Y. (n.d.) *5 tricks for an efficient morning at work*. Real Simple. http://www.wisnik.com/wp-content/uploads/2014/09/Real-Simple_TM_2014.pdf

9. Princeton University (2016). *Principles of effective time management for balance, well-being, and success*. The McGraw Center for Teaching & Learning. https://mcgraw.princeton.edu/sites/mcgraw/files/media/effective-time-management.pdf

10. Purdue University Global. (2018, April). *Time management tips for busy college students*. https://www.purdueglobal.edu/blog/student-life/time-management-busy-college-students/

11. Thomack, B. (2012). Time management for today's workplace demands. *Workplace Health & Safety, 60*(5), 201–203. https://doi.org/10.1177/216507991206000503

Problem-Solving and Decision Making

What These Are

These two sets of skills are heavily intertwined. In fact, decision making can be viewed as problem-solving when it is approached in a careful and systematic way. Skinner (1953) defines *problem-solving* as "any behavior which, through the manipulation of variables, makes the appearance of a solution more probable" (p. 584). Problem-solving involves several mediating responses including manipulating, supplementing, and generating stimuli (e.g., visualizing, questioning) to which an individual can subsequently respond (Axe et al,, 2019; Donahoe & Palmer, 2004; LeBlanc, Sellers et al., 2020; Skinner, 1953, 1957, 1968). Two common types of responses to problems do not qualify as problem-solving because they do not actually bring one closer to a solution: impulsivity and inactivity/avoidance (LeBlanc, n.d.; LeBlanc, Sellers et al. 2020). The supervisor can help supervisees and trainees overcome their tendencies to avoid noticing or reporting problems. The supervisor can

1. prompt the supervisee to monitor and report problems early,
2. respond positively when a supervisee reports a potential problem (e.g., praise the detection and report of the problem), and
3. model using a structured problem-solving approach to jointly solve problems.

LeBlanc, Sellers et al. (2020) and LeBlanc (n.d.) outline a five-step, structured problem-solving approach that can be used to make clinical decisions, solve staff performance problems, and tackle potential ethical dilemmas. The five steps should be followed in a systematic progression and the accuracy and effectiveness of performance at each step should be self-monitored. The five steps are:

1. detect the problem;
2. define the problem behaviorally;
3. generate solutions;
4. select a solution based on a pro/con analysis; and
5. implement the solution and evaluate the effects.

Step	Skill	Common Problem	Strategy to Increase Effectiveness
Detect the Problem	Nuanced Noticing—ability to notice subtle changes in behavior or the environment	Avoidance of early indicators of the problem Confusing the crisis with the underlying problem	Careful reflection Questioning
Define the Problem	Identify the functional determinants—A, B, Cs	Confusing topography with function Failure to generalize functional-assessment skills beyond client problem behavior	Functional-assessment interview Performance Diagnostic Checklist
Generate Potential Solutions	Brainstorming to produce a large and diverse set of potential solutions	Lack of variability in response generation Overuse of strategies that have worked in other situations No link between solution and functional determinants Evaluating and dismissing potential solutions (should not occur until step 4)	Brainstorm with two or more people. State expectations and goal for the number of options. Be ambitious with ideas. Change your environment. Specify how the solution addresses the function.
Select Solution(s)	Conduct a thorough analysis of the short-term and long-term pros and cons of at least two ideas.	Only identify pros of your own idea or cons of someone else's idea. Overfocus on short-term pros and cons Fail to recognize unintended impact of actions on others No solution is selected due to avoidance (i.e., I need more data, need to keep thinking about it)	Create a chart with short-term and long-term pros and cons. Seek input from those who might be impacted by the decision. Include taking no action as one of the options in your pro/con analysis.
Implement and Evaluate a Solution	Implementation Planning and Data Collection	Incomplete implementation planning No data collection on effects of the solution or on unintended consequences	Create an implementation plan with a timeline. Identify at least three metrics that might be expected to change based on the implementation.

This structured problem-solving model has been integrated into clinical decision-making models. The models guide the reader through a series of questions about the most common barriers to solution implementation (e.g., safety concerns, lack of resources) and the options that are best suited to overcome those barriers. These models then provide a pro/con analysis that assists the behavior analyst in collaborative decision making with the ultimate implementer (e.g., parent, teacher). For example, LeBlanc et al. (2016) describe a model for selecting appropriate measures for assessing and treating problem behavior. The model guides the user through questions about the topography of the behavior, environmental resources, and the importance of temporal dimensions for treatment planning. The answers to the questions in the model lead the user toward the measure(s) that are generally well-suited to the needs and constraints of the situation. The table provides a comprehensive pro/con analysis that allows the user to compare each reasonable option for the specific situation. Similarly, Geiger et al. (2010) provide a decision-making model and pro/con analysis for selecting function-based treatments for escape-maintained problem behavior and Grow et al. (2009) provide the same information for attention-maintained problem behavior.

The same structured problem-solving approach can be used to examine and solve ethical problems. LeBlanc, Onofrio et al. (2020) describe the development of an Ethics Network in a human service organization that was established to help employees conceptualize and respond to ethics scenarios using a structured problem-solving approach. They taught an overarching problem-solving strategy that was broadly applicable to many different ethical dilemmas. Their multistep, structured, problem-solving model included six steps, breaking the fifth step described above into two separate steps of implementation and evaluation. Throughout the organization, people were taught to analyze and respond to ethical scenarios using this approach.

Why They Are Important

Having a strong problem-solving repertoire is useful for both personal and professional situations (LeBlanc, Sellers, et al., 2020). Problems cause stress, anxiety, and avoidance in the absence of a framework for analysis and solution generation. Problems can also create the opportunity to hone problem-solving skills and develop confidence that enhances future problem-solving. "The supervisor who focuses on teaching problem-solving skills is programming for the supervisee's future independence and success by teaching them how to solve future problems, rather than simply providing a solution to the current problem" (LeBlanc, Sellers et al., 2020, p. 117). As we practice our problem-solving skills, we can overcome avoidance responses and tackle problems with confidence that we can analyze the problem, generate potential solutions, evaluate the success of the chosen option, and change course if the first solution does not work. The goal of structured collaborative problem-solving during supervision is that the supervisee learns they should not be afraid if they do not have an immediate answer because they have developed the ability to find those answers through the problem-solving process.

Assessing These Skills

These skills can be assessed via direct observation in structured problem-solving exercises using the problem-solving worksheet from LeBlanc, Sellers et al. (2020).

They can also be assessed in vivo as problems arise in the context of ongoing practice and supervision. The trainee can also self-assess their own problem-solving patterns using *Appendix B: Assessing Common Difficulties with Problem Solving* in LeBlanc, Sellers et al. (2020). In addition, here are indicators that will help you determine the skill levels of your trainees or NSs.

Skill Level	New BCBA	Supervisees/Trainees
Not yet acquired	✓ Frequently or always panics or becomes angry when a problem or ethical dilemma is detected ✓ Frequently or always has difficulty generating multiple solutions to a problem ✓ Frequently or always selects solutions and clinical options without conducting a pro/con analysis or identifying the function of the problem ✓ Frequently or always avoids noticing problems ✓ Frequently or always avoids making decisions ✓ Is insecure about their decisions ✓ Relies on strategies that they have seen work before even if those strategies are ill-suited to the current context ✓ Cannot describe the variables that should be influencing their choices	✓ Has difficulty generating any solutions to a problem ✓ Avoids noticing or reporting problems to supervisor ✓ Same
Developing	✓ Frequently remains calm when a problem is detected ✓ Frequently notices problems early ✓ Can successfully complete the 5-step problem-solving process ✓ Frequently generates multiple potential solutions linked to the function of the problem ✓ Can describe the benefits of making a decision even when it is difficult ✓ Can describe what they would do if plan A does not work out ✓ Can describe the variables that should be influencing their clinical choices ✓ Can analyze ethical dilemmas using the problem-solving model	✓ Same

Teaching/Refining These Skills

Supervisors who use this structured problem-solving approach in their own work have the perfect opportunity to model the process for their supervisees and trainees across a variety of areas (e.g., staff performance problems, clinical decisions, ethical dilemmas). They can describe the steps while going through them using Chapter 7 Appendix A from LeBlanc, Sellers et al. (2020). The supervisor can explicitly describe that clinical decision making is problem-solving and should be approached in a systematic way and describe prior problem-solving efforts and the results that were obtained. The supervisor can describe common, subtle indicators for emerging problems such as strained therapeutic relationships, blurred boundaries in the relationship with a client and family, or staff dissatisfaction with the supervisory process. The supervisor can ask the supervisee open-ended questions about what things make them think that a current situation is going well or going poorly. A supervisor can also use video examples to illustrate subtle behaviors or environmental conditions that might indicate that a problem is brewing.

To teach effective problem definition and function identification, the supervisor can prompt the supervisee or trainee to identify the functional determinants of any problem that they bring to supervision (e.g., clinical problems, ethical concerns, parent adherence problems). When a supervisee or trainee expresses frustration with staff performance or parent procedural integrity, prompt them to operationalize the problem and then use a tool such as the PDC-HS or the self-assessment of therapeutic relationship skills in Chapter 9 of LeBlanc, Sellers et al. (2020) to examine the problem in terms of the functional determinants. The supervisor might help their supervisees and trainees to see clinical decision making as an instance of problem-solving by reviewing the articles described above (Geiger et al., 2010; LeBlanc et al., 2016) with the trainee, explaining the use of the table in Step 3 of problem-solving.

Finally, the supervisor should encourage the supervisee to view this problem-solving process as a safety net that will help them become more confident and competent at problem-solving. In addition, step 5 of the model creates the opportunity to talk about mistakes as valuable learning experiences that enhance future problem-solving (i.e., we learn what not to do as well as what to do). The supervisor might describe an instance when a strategy they felt certain would work failed and what the next steps were. The supervisor must create an environment that encourages and reinforces honesty about mistakes and problems that have been detected.

Reflection	Action

✓ Think about a time when you faced a problem and identified a successful solution.
  ◦ Did you use any of the five steps of the structured process?
  ◦ What was the outcome?
✓ Think about some of the common problems you have encountered in clinical practice and supervision and if your colleagues have shared encountering similar issues.
✓ Use Appendix B of LeBlanc, Sellers et al., (2020) to reflect on any potential difficulties you might have with problem-solving.
	✓ Review the entire Ethics Code for Behavior Analysts (BACB, 2020) for examples of ethical problem-solving.
	✓ Complete Appendix A of Chapter 7 LeBlanc, Sellers et al. (2020) – Problem Solving Worksheet with a variety of problems.
	✓ Use a clinical decision-making model to collaboratively select a measurement system or function-based treatment for problem behavior.
	✓ Identify a person who remains calm throughout problem-solving and interview them about their problem-solving approach.

Resources

1. Kieta, A.R., Cihon, T.M. & Abdel-Jalil, A. (2019). Problem solving from a behavioral perspective: Implications for behavior analysts and educators. *Journal of Behavioral Education, 28*, 275–300 (2019).

2. LeBlanc, L. A., (2020). *Nobody's perfect*. Retrieved on April 3, 2020 from https://www.aubreydaniels.com/media-center/nobodys-perfect

3. LeBlanc, L. A., Sellers, T. P., & Alai, S. (2020). *Building and sustaining meaningful and efective relationships as a supervisor and mentor*. Sloan Publishing.

4. Robbins, J. K. (2011). Problem solving, reasoning, and analytical thinking in a classroom environment. *The Behavior Analyst Today, 12*(1), 40–47.

5. Skinner, B. F. (1984). An operant analysis of problem solving. *Behavioral and Brain Sciences, 7*(4), 583–591.

Public Speaking and Professional Presentations

What These Are

For the purposes of practicing behavior analysts, we will adopt the meaning of public speaking offered by Friman (2014) as anytime speaking in front of an audience. Certainly, presenting at a conference is public speaking, but so is presenting at an Individual Education Plan meeting, conducting a training, and leading a meeting (Heinicke et al., 2022). Public speaking involves disseminating information about the profession, the science, or clinical practice for the purposes of increasing understanding, demonstrating how to do something, or solving a shared problem. Professional presentation is a component of public speaking that involves the sharing of information or data, usually visually, in the form of reports, slides, graphs, or videos.

Why They Are Important

Effective public speaking and presenting skills are the primary ways to disseminate information and train skills. The ability to clearly communicate through verbal behavior and the presentation of well-organized visual material is critical to the success of an independent clinical practitioner and supervisor. These skills can result in increased confidence in and access to services and can facilitate collaboration, problem-solving, and the acquisition of skills targeted in training. These skills are critical when interacting with caregivers, other professionals, funding sources, and trainees and colleagues. On the other hand, poor public speaking and presenting skills can result in distrust, misunderstanding, and ineffective training (Heinicke et al., 2022). Some common issues with public speaking include anxiety, presence of disfluencies (i.e., responses produced by the speaker that interrupt the flow of their vocal behavior), poor audience control (e.g., failing to effectively match one's vocal verbal behavior to their listener), over reliance on a script, and avoiding public speaking. (Heinicke et al., 2022). Common problems with presenting are related to the amount, (too much or not enough), organization or flow, and focus (too in-depth or too surface) of the information being shared. Another issue related to presenting information is related to the quality of the visual material (e.g., overly complicated or blurry diagrams and graphs, slides with too much text). All these issues can result in the audience disengaging from the content, as well as frustration and misunderstanding on the part of the audience and the speaker.

Assessing These Skills

Assessing skills related to public speaking and presenting may be difficult for a few reasons. If individuals are very nervous, they may avoid accepting opportunities to speak publicly and supervisors may be reluctant to provide these opportunities, or they may simply not be available. One way to begin to assess these skills is to ask the individual how they feel about public speaking and what they perceive their skills to be. Attending to how individuals perform in individual, small, and large group meetings can also provide some measure of these skills. For example, if they rarely participate and when they do, they struggle to communicate their thoughts or questions in an organized manner, that may be an indicator that they will need some additional instruction and support to develop the related skills. Another option is to assign small, low stakes practice presentations and evaluate things such as presence of disfluencies, rate of speech and breathing, tone of voice, general affect, organization of the material, and use of visuals. Heinicke et al., 2022) provide a form in the appendices for evaluating public speaking that could be used to assess or self-assess public-speaking skills.

The indicators below will be most relevant to new BCBAs. These indicators may be relevant to supervisees who have roles that include the expectation to engage in public speaking and presenting (e.g., staff training, caregiver training, interviewing applicants). For trainees, these indicators may be helpful as they advance through their experience hours and get closer to independent practice.

Skill Level	New BCBA	Supervisees/Trainees
Not yet acquired	✓ Avoidance or refusal to engage in public speaking or presenting ✓ Infrequently or never able to clearly communicate intended information through public speaking or presenting ✓ Unable to engage in public speaking and presenting to a wide range of audiences (e.g., caregivers, supervisees and trainees, peers, other professionals) and for a variety of purposes (dissemination, sharing information, training) ✓ Infrequently or never identifies visual supports that may be helpful to present information ✓ Infrequently or never produces an outline of material in an organized manner ✓ Infrequently or never produces adequate or generally organized visual supports for a presentation	✓ Low or no participation in team meetings or staff training ✓ Infrequently or never expresses questions or comments in a succinct and organized manner ✓ Infrequently or never clearly communicates across a variety of audiences and topics ✓ Infrequently or never identifies visual supports that may be helpful to present information ✓ Infrequently or never outlines material in an organized manner

Skill Level	New BCBA	Supervisees/Trainees
Developing	✓ Hesitant acceptance to engage in formal public speaking or presenting but able to request assistance ✓ Frequently communicates some information through public speaking or presenting, likely relying on scripts or other prompts with success ✓ Able to engage in public speaking and presenting to a few different audiences (e.g., caregivers, supervisees and trainees, peers, other professionals) and for a few different purposes (dissemination, sharing information, training) ✓ Frequently identifies some visuals supports may be helpful to present information ✓ Frequently outlines material in an organized manner	✓ Consistent, active participation in team meetings or staff training ✓ Frequently expresses questions or comments in a succinct and organized manner ✓ Frequently communicates across a few audiences and topics with success ✓ Frequently identifies some visual supports that may be helpful to present information ✓ Frequently outlines material in a somewhat organized manner

Teaching These Skills

As with many skills, public speaking and presenting skills can be expressly taught with BST. Depending on an individual's skill level, it may be important to break the task of public speaking and presenting into component skills, or identify specific barriers, and focus on those. For example, if an individual engages in high levels of disfluencies or a very slow rate of speech, it may be worth focusing on reducing disfluencies or increasing rate of speech before focusing on creating and delivering a public presentation. Some strategies to consider include frequent practice opportunities in small and large group settings, using visual and auditory cues to influence rates of speech and frequency of disfluencies, and identifying a core message with which the audience can connect. For presenting skills, some strategies include making an outline of the content, selecting visuals that can help the audience connect with the material, and minimizing the amount of text on slides. Another strategy is to have individuals give short presentations on familiar topics to their peers and provide feedback to one another using a structured checklist. Finally, if individuals use PowerPoint, consider teaching them to use the design tools, particularly the "design ideas" feature for an individual slide.

Friman offers 15 steps to increasing one's public speaking skills in his 2014 article. Heinicke et al. (2022) provide specific strategies for teaching and improving public speaking and presentation skills that can be used to support teaching these skills. The authors also include a sample public feedback speaking form for evaluating and gathering feedback and a public speaking preparation checklist. Most importantly, for supervisors and mentors, they provide specific considerations and ideas across the BST components of describing, modeling, and practicing with feedback (Appendix C: Considerations for Supervisors/Mentors).

Reflection	Action
✓ Think about the physical and covert responses you have when thinking about or engaging in public speaking and presenting. ✓ Think about activities that you can engage in to reduce anxiety or stress related to public speaking and presenting (e.g., relaxation activities, practicing, co-presenting). ✓ Think about why being an effective public speaker is important.	✓ Identify and watch individuals who are excellent public speakers and presenters, paying close attention to what they do that is effective. ✓ Use self-management to set goals for yourself (e.g., identify a specific number of questions to ask or contributions to make in a meeting, decide that you will accept the next opportunity to engage in public speaking, ask for an opportunity). ✓ Create an opportunity to practice with peers, friends, or family. ✓ Play games that require some form of public speaking or presenting (e.g., Pictionary, Telegraphs, Charades). ✓ Take a workshop, course, or join a group that focuses on public speaking (e.g., Toastmasters, an improvisation class).

Resources

1. Effective Presentations Inc. (2019). *Public speaking training workshops, classes and coaching.* https://www.effectivepresentations.com/public/public-speaking-training

2. Friman, P. C. (2014). Behavior analysts to the front! A 15-step tutorial on public speaking. *The Behavior Analyst, 37,* 109–118. https://doi.org/10.1007/s40614-014-0009-y

3. Glassman, L. H., Forman, E. M., Herbert, J. D., Bradley, L. E., Foster, E. E., Izzetoglu, M., & Rocco, A. C. (2016). The effects of a brief acceptance-based behavioral treatment versus traditional cognitive-behavioral treatment for public speaking anxiety: An exploratory trial examining differential effects on performance and neurophysiology. *Behavior Modification, 40,* 748–776. https://doi.org/10.1177/0145445516629939

4. Heinicke, M. R., Juanico, J. F., Valentino, A. L., & Sellers, T. P. (2022). Improving behavior analysts' public speaking: Recommendations from expert interviews. *Behavior Analysis in Practice, 15,* 203-218.

5. Laborda, M. A., Schofield, C. A., Johnson, E. M., Schubert, J. R., George-Denn, D., Coles, M. E., & Miller, R. R. (2016). The extinction and return of fear of public speaking. *Behavior Modification, 40,* 901–921. https://doi.org/10.1177/0145445516645766

6. Mancuso, C., & Miltenberger, R. G. (2016). Using habit reversal to decrease filled pauses in public speaking. *Journal of Applied Behavior Analysis, 49,* 1–5. https://doi.org/10.1002/jaba.267

7. Mladenka, J. D., Sawyer, C. R., & Behnke, R. R. (1998). Anxiety sensitivity and speech trait anxiety as predictors of state anxiety during public speaking. *Communication Quarterly, 46,* 417–429. https://doi.org/10.1080/01463379809370112

8. Montes, C. C., Heinicke, M. R., & Geierman, D. M. (2019). Awareness training reduces college students' speech disfluencies in public speaking. *Journal of Applied Behavior Analysis, 52,* 746–755. https://doi.org/10.1002/jaba.569

9. North, M. (2019). *10 Tips For Improving Your Public Speaking Skills.* Harvard extension school professional development blog. https://www.extension.harvard.edu/professional-development/blog/10-tips-improving-your-public-speaking-skills

10. O'Hair, D., Rubenstein, H., & Stewart, R. (2015). *A pocket guide to public speaking.* Bedford/St. Martin's.

11. Spieler, C., & Miltenberger, R. (2017). Using awareness training to decrease nervous habits during public speaking. *Journal of Applied Behavior Analysis, 50,* 38–47. https://doi.org/10.1002/jaba.362

12. Toastmasters. (2019). *All about toastmasters.* https://www.toastmasters.org/about/all-about-toastmasters/

13. Valentino, A. L., LeBlanc, L. A., & Sellers, T. P. (2016). The benefits of group supervision and a recommended structure for implementation. *Behavior Analysis in Practice, 9,* 320–328. https://doi.org/10.1007/s40617-016-0138-8

Scope Of Competence

What This Is

Let's start by first describing scope of practice. Brodhead et al. (2018) note that scope of practice is used to indicate the constellation of activities appropriate for individuals in a profession to practice based on a certification, credential, or license. Scope of competence generally refers to a professional's ability to consistently perform a skill or task effectively and accurately, typically meeting some predetermined expectation or criterion. In the Ethics Code for Behavior Analysts, scope of competence is defined as "The professional activities a behavior analyst can consistently perform with proficiency." (BACB, 2020, p. 8). In summary, scope of practice is defined for the profession by oversight organizations (e.g., BACB, licensure boards), whereas scope of competence is measured at the individual professional level (e.g., BCBA, BCaBA, RBT, trainee).

Why This Is Important

It is critical for each BCBA to understand their own scope of competence at a given point in their career, and to continually evaluate it, to maximize benefits and avoid causing harm. The quality of ABA services and outcomes are directly dependent on the skill level of the service providers. Inadequate service delivery, whether clinical services or supervision and training, has serious risks for the recipients. Low-quality clinical services can result in lost time due to delayed progress with acquisition or behavior reduction interventions, worsening of behavior of concerns, and risk of physical and emotional harm to consumers. Poor training and supervision can result in skill deficits for trainees and supervisees, as well as all the previously listed risk for consumers. ABA services are evidence-based and driven by existing and ever-progressing research. Therefore, it is incumbent on BCBAs to continually evaluate, maintain, and adjust their skills to remain in line with current practice recommendations. Furthermore, BCBAs providing supervision to supervisees and trainees must also teach them how to evaluate their scope of competence.

Assessing This Skill

The ability to accurately describe and evaluate one's own scope of competence can be assessed by having discussions about what scope of competence is and the factors that should be considered when evaluating one's scope of competence. The primary function of being able to fully understand one's own scope of competence is to ensure that one practices only within this scope, as practicing outside it invites risk of harm. Therefore, another activity to assist in assessing this skill is to present a variety of case examples with a wide range of settings, populations, presenting needs, and assessment and intervention technologies and asking the individual if they feel competent to independently provide services for the case example. If they indicate that they do, ask them to describe the training and experience they have that makes them competent. If they indicate they are not competent, ask them to list why and to describe the action(s) they would take if they wanted to expand their scope of competence. Alligood and Gravina (2021) and LeBlanc et al. (2012) provide specific strategies for expanding one's area of practice and scope of competence.

Use the indicators in the table below to assess if an individual has yet begun acquiring skills related to evaluating their scope of competence, or if the skills are emerging.

Skill Level	New BCBA	Supervisees/Trainees
Not yet acquired	✓ Unable to describe scope of competence, why it is important, and the associate risks of failing to practice with one's scope of competence ✓ Unable to describe the factors to consider when evaluating one's scope of competence ✓ Infrequently or never identifies resources related to scope of competence ✓ Indicating that they can or should be able to engage in certain tasks for which they do not have proper training ✓ Engaging in practices and activities without the proper training ✓ Delegating practices and tasks to others who lack proper training	✓ Unable to describe scope of competence, why it is important, and the associate risks of failing to practice with one's scope of competence ✓ Infrequently or never identifies resources related to scope of competence ✓ Indicating that they can or should be able to engage in certain tasks for which they do not have proper training ✓ Engaging in practices and activities without the proper training, particularly without asking a supervisor
Developing	✓ Able to provide a sufficient description of scope of competence, but might not have full understanding of the associated importance or risks ✓ Frequently identifies resources (e.g., ethics standards, articles) ✓ Able to describe some of the factors to consider when evaluating ✓ Able to accurately identify some practices within and outside of their own and other's scope of competence ✓ Appropriately seeking out guidance related to scope of competence ✓ Appropriately delegating some practices and tasks to others ✓ Appropriately withholding some tasks from others	✓ Able to provide an emerging or accurate description of scope of competence ✓ Frequently identifies related ethics standards ✓ Able to accurately describe some tasks within and outside of their scope of competence ✓ Appropriately seeking support from supervisor when concerned about practicing outside of scope of competence

Teaching This Skill

In taking a BST approach to teaching the skill of evaluating one's scope of competence should include a discussion of the skill, modeling the skill, and rehearsing the skill with feedback until mastery. When describing the skill, be sure to include the following points:

1. BACB ethics standards,
2. the benefits,
3. the risks, and
4. the idea that this is a continual practice throughout one's career.

You can model the skill throughout your supervisory relationship and in clinical settings by describing a) how and when you self-assess, and b) your scope of competence in relation to accepting or not accepting clients, supervisees, and trainees. The rehearsal component should include a variety of role-plays with case scenarios to which individuals can indicate

a. if they have the relevant competence,
b. why or why not,
c. the risks of accepting the client if the needs are outside of their scope, and
d. actions they might take if the client's needs were outside their scope (e.g., refer out, co-treat, gain the skills via training or consultation).

Use the reflection activities together with your NS or by yourself to support your skills in evaluating and identifying your scope of competence or to work on increasing scope of competence.

Reflection	Action

✓ Reflect on the definition of scope of competence, its importance, and risks.
✓ Reflect on what thoughts and feelings come up around the topic of scope of competence.
✓ Reflect on your training contexts and the degree to which you received high-quality training and supervision.
✓ Reflect on whether you were trained to competency.
✓ Reflect on the skills and activities you regularly engage in, and those with which you might be rusty.
✓ Reflect on whether anyone has ever talked to you about their scope of competence, and if so
  ◦ What was the context (e.g., indicating something was within or outside their scope of competence)?
  ◦ What did they say?
  ◦ How did the conversation make you feel?
✓ Reflect on whether anyone has expressly trained you how to evaluate scope of competence.
✓ Reflect on whether you can recall an instance where you think you or someone else may have acted outside of your scope of competence, the outcome, and if you would do anything differently now.
	✓ Make a list of the following variables relative to your work experience: populations worked with, settings worked in, assessment and intervention procedures designed and completed, clinical practices engaged in (e.g., report writing, interviewing), supervising and training, performance monitoring and management.
	✓ Now go back and add in the following for each of the above variables: observed, assisted, trained to predetermined competency, completed independently, trained others.
	✓ For any variables you indicated independence completion and/or trained others write the number of consecutive years (e.g., working a given population, implementing a given intervention technology) and number of months/years since (if applicable).
	✓ Review the related standards in the Ethics Code for Behavior Analysts and the RBT Ethics Code.
	✓ Read articles and discuss.
	✓ Complete the self-assessment in Brodhead et al. (2018).
	✓ Calendar time to engage in regular (e.g., quarterly) self-evaluation of your scope of competence until it becomes fluent.

Resources

1. Alligood, C. A., & Gravina, N. E. (2021). Branching out: Finding success in new areas of practice. *Behavior Analysis in Practice, 14*(1), 283-289.

2. Briggs, A. M., & Mitteer, D. R. (2021). Updated strategies for making regular contact with the scholarly literature. *Behavior Analysis in Practice*, 1-12.

3. Brodhead, M. T., Quigley, S. P., & Wilczynski, S. M. (2018). A call for discussion about scope of competence in behavior analysis. *Behavior Analysis In Practice, 11*(4), 424-435.

4. Carr, J. E., & Briggs, A. M. (2010). Strategies for making regular contact with the scholarly literature. *Behavior Analysis In Practice, 3*(2), 13-18.

5. LeBlanc, L. A., Heinicke, M. R., & Baker, J. C. (2012). Expanding the consumer base for behavior-analytic services: Meeting the needs of consumers in the 21st century. *Behavior Analysis in Practice, 5*(1), 4-14.

6. LeBlanc, L. A., Sellers, T. P., & Ala'i, S. (2020). *Building and sustaining meaningful and effective relationships as a supervisor and mentor.* Sloan Publishing.

Self-Care

What This Is

Figley (2002) described *self-care* as actively engaging practices or behavior focused on facilitating quality of life and managing work-life balance. Self-care typically involves engaging in self-monitoring to assess one's behavior and needs and self-management to enact plans for improvement of self-care practices. Self-care practices must be individualized, and they are specifically tied to one's history, intersecting cultural identity, and current context. However, self-care practices typically involve evaluating and engaging in behaviors in the following areas: physical health, emotional/psychological health, spiritual practices, personal and social behavior, and professional and workplace behavior.

Why This Is Important

The work of a clinician is exciting and valuable. At the same time, it can be stressful and produce burnout (Plantiveau et al., 2018). Burnout can produce diminished enjoyment of an individual's work and can invite drifting from high-quality practices resulting in less-optimal outcomes for, and possible harm to clients, caregivers, supervisees, and trainees. Burnout may impact some individuals so severely that they choose to leave the profession. Actively self-assessing and managing self-care needs and practices can increase an individual's ability to manage stress and work-life balance and can facilitate a reinforcing and sustained career in behavior analysis.

Assessing This Skill

Self-care skills can be assessed in a number of ways. Supervisors, managers, and mentors should continually engage in careful observation of individuals to detect indicators of stress (e.g., fatigue, changes in affect and quality of work, statements of being overwhelmed). Regular check-ins during meetings provide the perfect opportunity to ask questions and have meaningful discussions around stress levels, work-life balance, and self-care activities. Chapters 7, 8, 9, 10, and 11 in the LeBlanc, Sellers et al. (2020) book provide recommendations and resources for assessing repertoires that are often related to, or provide an indication of, increased stress (e.g., organization and time management, issues in the supervisory relationship). One only needs to enter the terms "self-care assessment" or "assessing stress" into a search engine to find a number of helpful tools for assessing self-care and levels of stress that can be used as self-assessments or to facilitate discussions about assessing an individual's stress levels and self-care practices. For example, the Boston School of Social Work Center for Innovation in Social Work & Health provides free online access to the *Self-Assessment Tool: Self-Care*, a .PDF that provides structured self-rating items across the areas of physical, psychological, emotional, spiritual, and workplace/professional self-care (Boston School of Social Work, n.d.).

Skill Level	New BCBA	Supervisees/Trainees
Not yet acquired	✓ Frequent statements related to feeling unable to manage workload or work-life balance. ✓ Frequent statements that work is not reinforcing or fun. ✓ Frequent disruptions to work; activities seemingly related to stress (e.g., frequent cancellations and missed deadlines). ✓ Activity level is a frequent barrier to completing tasks (e.g., low or high energy results in poor follow-through). ✓ Frequent emotional responding in a variety of contexts (e.g., crying, snapping at people). ✓ Rarely or never says no to opportunities or tasks. ✓ Rarely or never asks for support.	✓ Same
Developing	✓ Some statements indicating identification they need to take action to manage workload or work-life balance. ✓ Scheduling planned time off. ✓ Moderate to infrequent disruptions to work activities and tacting when they are relating difficulty managing workload, stress, or work-life balance. ✓ Some active management of activity level (e.g., engaging strategies to elevate activity level or manage distractions). ✓ Moderate to infrequent emotional responding; when emotional responding occurs strategies to mediate are implemented; strategies are implemented to minimize emotional responding (e.g., scripts and practice for difficult conversation, breathing activities).	✓ Same

Teaching This Skill

Supervisors should focus on teaching supervisees and trainees how to engage in frequent self-assessment and self-reflection related to self-care and stress management, as well as how to create and manage a plan for self-care. This is likely best accomplished through discussion and practice; however, it is critical to follow the lead of the individual in these endeavors. Some individuals may feel comfortable discussing the topics and exploring tools but may not feel comfortable completing the self-assessments or self-care planning collaboratively with their supervisor. Therefore, emphasis should be placed on discussion, reviewing resources and tools, frequent check-ins, and the offer to practice or support the individual in the development of a self-care plan, goals, and activities. Regardless of the degree of collaboration, highlighting the use of self-monitoring, self-reflection, and self-management practices to support self-care will be critical. LeBlanc,

Sellers et al. (2020) provide descriptions of these practices and resources to support them in chapters 2, 3, 4, and 6, and offer additional guidance in skills-specific chapters related to subjects such as problem-solving and organization and time management. They also include strategies for taking an active approach to planning for a sustained and rewarding career in chapter 12. Fiebig et al. (2020) describe strategies and resources for engaging in self-care activities, includes activities to identify and clarify values that can support engaging in self-care practices.

Reflection	Action
✓ Spend some time thinking about your feelings and private events related to your typical work and life activities. ✓ Think about work and life activities that bring you joy and those that cause frustration or discomfort and reflect on possible barriers (e.g., lack of resources or skills). ✓ Think about how you feel and behave when your work or life stressors are well managed and when they are not well managed; how you think others are impacted in each situation.	✓ Write down words that describe how you feel about your work and life (e.g., energized, exhausted, frustrated). ✓ Complete a self-care, self-compassion, or compassion-fatigue self-assessment. ✓ Make a recipe that describes the ingredients needed for you to perform at your best in work and life activities (e.g., minimal number of hours of sleep or exercise, minimal frequency engaging in hobbies, leisure, or social activities, minimal support needed from managers or supervisors, necessary resources). ✓ Create a self-management plan focusing on goals for your self-care.

Resources

1. Boston School of Social Work Center for Innovation in Social Work & Health (n.d.). *Self assessment tool: Self-care.* https://www.ucebt.com/images/pdfs-doc/SelfAssessmentToolSelfCare-PeerRole-Peer_Training.pdf\

2. Fiebig, J. H., Gould, E. R., Ming, S., & Watson, R. A. (2020). An invitation to act on the value of self-care: Being a whole person in all that you do. *Behavior Analysis in Practice, 13*(3):559-567.doi: 10.1007/s40617-020-00442-x.

3. Figley, C. R. (2002). Compassion fatigue: Psychotherapists' chronic lack of self-care. *Journal of Clinical Psychology, 58*(11), 1433-1441.

4. LeBlanc, L. A., Sellers, T. P., & Ala'i, S. (2020). *Building and sustaining meaningful and effective relationships as a supervisor and mentor.* Sloan Publishing.

5. Plantiveau, C., Dounavi, K., & Virués-Ortega, J. (2018). High levels of burnout among early career board-certified behavior analysts with low collegial support in the work environment. *European Journal of Behavior Analysis, 19*(2), 195-207.

Teaching Effectively Using BST

What This Is

Parsons et al. (2012) describe this competency-based training method as including the six following steps:

1. providing a description of the skill (i.e., verbal instruction),
2. giving a written/visual description of the skill (i.e., written instruction including job aids),
3. demonstrating the skill (i.e., modeling),
4. providing practice opportunities (i.e., rehearsal),
5. providing feedback on the performance during rehearsal, and
6. repeating those 5 steps until the desired performance criterion is reached.

Miltenberger (2015) describes BST as including four main components:

1. instructions,
2. modeling,
3. rehearsal, and
4. feedback until a performance criterion is reached.

Regardless of whether you break BST into 4 or 6 steps, this type of training places importance on direct performance opportunities and continuation of training until new skills are repeatedly demonstrated through accurate performance. Without rehearsal and feedback opportunities, most people will be unable to consistently perform at a high level after training is completed (i.e., skill maintenance).

Instructions. This step involves providing a clear description of the skill with detail about each component and why it is important. The information should be presented in manageable chunks and the rationales should focus on the benefits of implementing the skill correctly, the risks of error, and any nuances associated with each skill. The vocal and written instructions should be clear and concise. They may include a job aid, which is a permanently available concisely written description of a task in the form of a checklist, summary sheet, flowchart, or screen capture (LeBlanc, Sellers et al., 2020). This component is often combined or alternated with the next component: modeling.

Modeling. Modeling involves demonstration of the target skill and can take the form of a live demonstration or video model. If the demonstration is live, it should be carefully scripted in advance. The models should include multiple exemplars of correct implementation of the skill. Video models may also allow demonstration of the skill with multiple people and in multiple contexts. The demonstration should begin with a simple version of the skill with increased complexity in later demonstrations. In addition, the supervisor may alternate providing instructions and modeling components if a skill is complicated and involves multiple steps (i.e., instructions and modeling for step 1, instructions and modeling for step 2, instructions and modeling for step 3, rehearsal of steps 1-3).

Rehearsal. The rehearsal component involves actively practicing the target skill in a role-play or natural context. The practice activities should proceed from simple to more complex with introduction of distractors and disruptors (e.g., prompting, collecting data, addressing problem behavior) before the skill is considered finally mastered. The new skills may initially be rehearsed at a much slower pace and with extensive use of the job aids to ensure that the person being trained has an opportunity to perform correctly and encounter reinforcement. This step is often interspersed with the following step: feedback. That is, during or after each practice opportunity, the trainer typically provides supportive and corrective feedback followed by another opportunity to practice the skill.

Feedback. Feedback refers to providing information about some specific aspect of the performance in comparison to some criterion. Feedback is one of the most powerful tools we have for shaping and maintaining a supervisee's performance. In the context of initial training, it is important to provide feedback about each aspect of the performance in a way that corresponds to the prior instruction. That is, if you described 4 components of the skill, you should provide feedback on the rehearsal performance for each of those 4 components. If three were performed accurately, praise the success for each of these as well as pointing out errors on the other component. Generally, feedback is provided immediately during initial training trials and the delay is gradually increased by the end of training when performance is highly accurate. See the Skill Section on Feedback for additional detail about the specific delivery of feedback.

Repeated Practice Until Competent. The steps and components outlined above are subject to evaluation of their effectiveness. Although this procedure has a strong evidence base to support its effectiveness in general, the trainer should be evaluating the effects of their unique implementation of BST on the performance of the person they are training. Throughout practice and feedback, data should be collected on the accuracy of the skill. That performance should be evaluated against a success criterion, exactly as we would do when teaching a client a new skill. The criterion will vary based on the complexity and importance of the skill, but the criterion should specify a minimum acceptable level of accuracy (e.g., 90% accuracy) and stability (e.g., across 2 practice sessions) for performance. Training should not be considered complete until that success criterion has been reached.

Why This Is Important

Both the Ethics Code for Behavior Analysts (BACB, 2020) and the Supervisor Training Curriculum Outline 2.0 (BACB, 2020) specify that behavior analysts should implement effective training. Behavioral skills training (BST) is an effective and evidence-based training strategy (Parsons et al., 2012; Miltenberger, 2015) that has been investigated across a wide range of target skills. This approach stands in stark contrast to traditional classroom instruction where instructions are provided for a pre-determined amount of time but there is no demonstration that the skill has been acquired. Though it is more effortful than the traditional model, it is also more effective. It is important to include all components of BST because without rehearsal and feedback opportunities, most people will be unable to consistently perform at a high level after training is completed (i.e., skill maintenance).

Assessing These Skills

These skills can be assessed through permanent product, role-play, and in vivo performance. For example, trainees could submit permanent products such as a PowerPoint presentation for the instructions, a job aid, or a data sheet to use during rehearsal.

For role-playing delivery of the instructions and implementation or rehearsal and feedback, group supervision might provide an opportunity for trainees to serve as the trainer in some role-plays and as the learner in other role-plays. The assignment could focus on a particular component (e.g., creating a job aid, creating a video model) but it is important to assess the ability to implement all components of BST eventually.

Skill Level	New BCBA	Supervisees/Trainees
Not yet acquired	✓ Instructions may be overly complex or lack detail. ✓ No rationale is given, or the rationale does not adequately convey the importance of accuracy and the risk of error. ✓ Trainee infrequently or never creates an effective job aid ✓ Models do not capture the critical components of the skill or do not illustrate multiple exemplars. ✓ Training is considered complete without demonstration of accurate performance. ✓ Feedback is non-specific or overly focused on errors. ✓ No success criterion is used.	✓ Same
Developing	✓ Instructions are brief and concise ✓ The rationale accurately and clearly conveys the importance of the skill and correct performance. ✓ Job aids contain crisp visuals that aid performance. ✓ Multiple models are used during training. ✓ Models illustrate the critical components of the skill. ✓ Rehearsal and feedback are repeated until a success criterion is met. ✓ Feedback focuses on accurate performance as well as errors. ✓ Feedback is delivered in an acceptable and compassionate manner.	✓ Same

Teaching These Skills

These skills are foundational to effective supervision and should be covered in academic coursework related to supervision and personnel management. However, academic coursework alone is unlikely to produce a robust repertoire for training others. It is important to review the content from coursework as a form of instruction, model the use of BST as you teach the trainee various other skills (e.g., active listening, ethical decision making), and allow opportunities to practice the component skills until mastery. That is, use BST to teach your trainees how to use BST.

Reflection	Action
✓ Think about a prior teacher, supervisor, coach, or trainer who was very effective at teaching you something. Did they use any of the components of BST? ✓ Think about a prior teacher, supervisor, coach, or trainer who was not effective at teaching you something. Which of the components of BST were missing in their instruction?	✓ Review the relevant standards (4.06, 4.08, and 4.10) from the Ethics Code for Behavior Analysts (BACB, 2020). ✓ Identify a skill that you think would be easy to teach using BST and create the materials. ✓ Identify a skill that you think would be hard to teach using BST and describe what would be hard about it.

Resources

1. LeBlanc, L. A., Sellers, T. P., & Ala'i, S. (2020). *Building and sustaining meaningful and effective relationships as a supervisor and mentor*. Sloan Publishing.

2. Miltenberger, R. G. (2015). *Behavior modification: Principles and procedures* (6th Edition). Cengage.

3. Parsons, M. B., Rollyson, J. H., & Reid, D. H. (2012). *Evidence-based staff training. Behavior Analysis In Practice, 5*, 2–11. doi: 10.1007/BF03391819

References

Allen, D. A. (2015). *Getting things done: The art of stress-free productivity* (Revised). Penguin Publishing.

Allen, D. A., & Hall, B. (2019). *The getting things done workbook: 10 moves to stress-free productivity*. Platkus.

Alligood, C. A., & Gravina, N. E. (2021). Branching out: Finding success in new areas of practice. *Behavior Analysis in Practice, 14*(1), 283-289.

Axe, J. B., Phelan, S. H., & Irwin, C. L. (2019). Empirical evaluations of Skinner's problem- solving analysis. *The Analysis of Verbal Behavior, 35*(1), 39–56. doi.org/10.1007/s40616-018-0103-4

Bailey, J., & Burch, M. (2010). *25 Essential skills & strategies for the professional behavior analyst*. Routledge.

Bandura, A. B. (1997). *Self-efficacy: The exercise of control*. W. H. Freeman.

Behavior Analyst Certification Board. (2020). *Ethics code for behavior analysts*. Author.

Behavior Analyst Certification Board (2021). https://www.bacb.com/wp-content/uploads/2020/11/Consultation-Supervisor-Requirements-and-Documentation_210528.pdf

Boston School of Social Work Center for Innovation in Social Work & Health (n.d.). *Self- assessment tool: Self-care*. https://www.ucebt.com/images/pdfs-doc/SelfAssessmentToolSelfCare-PeerRole-Peer_Training.pdf\

Brodhead, M. T., Quigley, S. P., & Wilczynski, S. M. (2018). A call for discussion about scope of competence in behavior analysis. *Behavior Analysis in Practice, 11*(4), 424-435.

Carr, J. E., Wilder, D. A., Majdalany, L., Mathisen, D., & Strain, L. A. (2013). An assessment- based solution to a human-service employee performance problem. *Behavior Analysis in Practice, 6*, 16–32.

Chase, J. A., Houmanfar, R., Hayes, S. C., Ward, T.A., Vilardaga, J.P., & Follette, V. (2013). Values are not just goals: Online act-based values training adds to goal setting in improving undergraduate college student performance. *Journal of Contextual Behavioral Science, 2*(3-4), 79-84.

Conners, B., Johnson, A., Duarte, J., Murriky, R., & Marks, K. (2019). Future directions of training and fieldwork in diversity issues in applied behavior analysis. *Behavior Analysis in Practice, 12*(4), 767–776. https://doi.org/10.1007/s40617-019-00349-2

Conners, B., & Capell, S. T (2020). *Multiculturalism and diversity in applied behavior analysis* 1st edition. Routledge.

Coyne, L. W., Gould, E. R., Grimaldi, M., Wilson, K. G., Baffuto, G., & Biglan, A. (2021). First things first: Parent psychological flexibility and self-compassion during covid-19. *Behavior Analysis in Practice, 14*(4), 1092-1098.

Donahoe, J. W., & Palmer, D. C. (2004). *Learning and complex behavior*. Boston: Allyn & Bacon.

Ehrlich, R. J., Nosik, M. R., Carr, J. E., & Wine, B. (2020). Teaching employees how to receive feedback: A preliminary investigation. *Journal of Organizational Behavior Management, 40*(1-2), 19-29.

Ervin, N. E. (2008). Caseload management skills for improved efficiency. *The Journal of Continuing Education in Nursing, 39*(3), 127–132.

Fiebig, J. H., Gould, E. R., Ming, S., & Watson, R. A. (2020). An invitation to act on the value of self-care: Being a whole person in all that you do. *Behavior Analysis in Practice, 13*(3), 559-567. doi: 10.1007/s40617-020-00442-x.

Fienup, D. M., Luiselli, J. K., Joy, M., Smyth, D., & Stein, R. (2013). Organizational behavior change: Improving the timeliness of staff meetings at a human services organization. *Journal of Organizational Behavior Management, 33*, 252–264. https://doi.org/10.1080/01608061.2013.843435

Figley, C. R. (2002). Compassion fatigue: Psychotherapists' chronic lack of self-care. *Journal of Clinical Psychology, 58*(11), 1433-1441.

Fisher-Borne, M., Cain, J. M., & Martin, S. L. (2015). From mastery to accountability: Cultural humility as an alternative to cultural competence. *Social Work Education, 34*(2), 165–181.

Fong, E. H., Catagnus, R. M., Brodhead, M. T., Quigley, S., & Field, S. (2016). Developing the cultural awareness skills of behavior analysts. *Behavior Analysis in Practice, 9*(1), 84–94. https://doi.org/10.1007/s40617-016-0111-6

Friman, P. C. (2014). Behavior analysts to the front! A 15-step tutorial on public speaking. *The Behavior Analyst, 37*, 109–118. https://doi.org/10.1007/s40614-014-0009-y

Garza, K. L., McGee, H. M., Schenk, Y. A., & Wiskirchen, R. R. (2018). Some tools for carrying out a proposed process for supervising experience hours for aspiring Board-Certified Behavior Analysts®. *Behavior Analysis in Practice, 11*, 62–70.

Geiger, K. A., Carr, J. E., & LeBlanc, L. A. (2010). Function-based treatments for escape-maintained problem behavior: A treatment selection model for practicing behavior analysts. *Behavior Analysis in Practice, 3*, 22–32.

Gravina, N., Villacorta, J., Albert, K., Clark, R., Curry, S., & Wilder, D. (2018). A literature review of organizational behavior management interventions in human service settings from 1990 to 2016. *Journal of Organizational Behavior Management, 38*(23), 191–224. doi:10.1080/01608061.2018.1454872

Grenny, J., Patterson, K., McMillan, R., Switzler, A., & Gregory, E. (2022). *Crucial conversations: Tools for talking when stakes are high* (3rd ed.). McGraw Hill.

Grow, L. L., Carr, J. E., & LeBlanc, L. A. (2009). Treatments for attention-maintained problem behavior: Empirical support and clinical recommendations. *Journal of Evidence-Based Practices for Schools, 10*, 70–92.

Heinicke, M. R., Juanico, J. F., Valentino, A. L., & Sellers, T. P. (in press). Improving behavior analysts' public speaking: Recommendations from expert interviews. *Behavior Analysis in Practice, 15*, 203-218.

Hook, J. N., Davis, D. E., Owen, J., Worthington Jr, E. L., & Utsey, S. O. (2013). Cultural humility: Measuring openness to culturally diverse clients. *Journal of Counseling Psychology, 60*(3), 353.

Kieta, A. R., Cihon, T. M. & Abdel-Jalil, A. (2019). Problem-solving from a behavioral perspective: Implications for behavior analysts and educators. *Journal of Behavioral Education, 28,* 275–300 (2019).

Kristensen, T. S., Borritz, M., Villadsen, E., & Christensen, K. B. (2005). The copenhagen burnout inventory: A new tool for the assessment of burnout. *Work & Stress, 19*(3), 192-207.

Leach, D. J., Rogelberg, S. J., Warr, P. B., & Burnfield, J. L. (2009). Perceived meeting characteristics: The role of design characteristics. *Journal of Business Psychology, 24,* 65–76. https://doi.org/10.1007/s10869-009-9092-6

LeBlanc, L. A., (2020). *Nobody's perfect.* Retrieved on April 3, 2020, from https://www.aubreydaniels.com/media-center/nobodys-perfect

LeBlanc, L. A., & Nosik, M. (2019). Planning and leading effective meetings. *Behavior Analysis in Practice, 12,* 696-708.

LeBlanc, L. A., Heinicke, M. R., & Baker, J. C. (2012). Expanding the consumer base for behavior-analytic services: Meeting the needs of consumers in the 21st century. *Behavior Analysis in Practice, 5*(1), 4-14.

LeBlanc, L. A., Sellers, T. P., & Ala'i, S. (2020). *Building and sustaining meaningful and effective relationships as a supervisor and mentor.* Sloan Publishing.

LeBlanc, L. A., Sleeper, J. D., Mueller, J. R., Jenkins, S. R., & Harper-Briggs, A. M. (2020). Assessing barriers to effective caseload management by practicing behavior analysts. *Journal of Organizational Behavior Management, 39*(3–4), 317–336.

LeBlanc, L. A., Taylor, B. A., & Marchese N. V. (2019). The training experiences of behavior analysts: Compassionate care and therapeutic relationships with caregivers. *Behavior Analysis in Practice, 13,* 387–393. https://doi.org/10.1007/s40617-019-00368-z

LeBlanc, L. A., Onofrio, O. M., Valentino A. L., & Sleeper, J. D. (2020). Promoting ethical discussions and decision making in a human service agency. *Behavior Analysis in Practice, 13,* 905-913.

Lencioni, P. (2004). *Death by meeting.* Jossey-Bass.

Miltenberger, R. G. (2015). *Behavior modification: Principles and procedures* (6th Edition). Cengage.

Parsons, M. B., Rollyson, J. H., & Reid, D. H. (2012). Evidence-based staff training. *Behavior Analysis in Practice, 5,* 2–11. doi: 10.1007/BF03391819

Plantiveau, C., Dounavi, K., & Virués-Ortega, J. (2018). High levels of burnout among early career board-certified behavior analysts with low collegial support in the work environment. *European Journal of Behavior Analysis, 19*(2), 195-207.

Robbins, J. K. (2011). Problem-solving, reasoning, and analytical thinking in a classroom environment. *The Behavior Analyst Today, 12*(1), 40–47.

Sellers, T. P., Valentino, A. L., & LeBlanc, L. A. (2016). Recommended practices for individual supervision of aspiring behavior analysts. *Behavior Analysis in Practice, 9*(4), 274-286.

Skinner, B. F. (1953). *Science and human behavior.* Macmillan.

Skinner, B. F. (1957). *Verbal behavior*. Prentice Hall.

Skinner, B. F. (1968). *The technology of teaching*. Appleton-Century-Crofts

Skinner, B. F. (1984). An operant analysis of problem-solving. *Behavioral and Brain Sciences, 7*(4), 583-591.

Taylor, B. A., LeBlanc, L. A., & Nosik, M. R. (2019). Compassionate care in behavior analytic treatment: Can outcomes be enhanced by attending to relationships with caregivers?. *Behavior Analysis in Practice, 12*, 654–666. https://doi.org/10.1007/s40617-018-0089-3

Turner, L. B., Fischer, A. J., & Luiselli, J. K. (2016). Towards a competency-based, ethical, and socially valid approach to the supervision of applied behavior analytic trainees. *Behavior Analysis in Practice, 9*(4), 287-298.

Walker, S., & Sellers, T. (2021). Teaching appropriate feedback reception skills using computer-based instruction: A systematic replication. *Journal of Organizational Behavior Management, 41*(3), 236-254.

Ward-Horner, J., & Sturmey, P. (2012). Component analysis of behavior skills training in functional analysis. *Behavioral Interventions, 27*(2), 75–92.

Wright, P. I. (2019). Cultural humility in the practice of applied behavior analysis. *Behavior Analysis in Practice, 12*, 805–809.

Appendix A: Yearly Planning Guide/Roadmap for New Supervisor

BCBA Initials:____					
Month 1	Planning Logistics and Building Relationships	Planning Logistics and Building Relationships	Planning Logistics and Building Relationships	Planning Logistics and Building Relationships	Planning Logistics and Building Relationships
Month 2	Assessing and Self Assessing	Assessing and Self Assessing	Assessing and Self Assessing	Assessing and Self Assessing	Assessing and Self Assessing
Month 3	Curricular Roadmap and Competencies	Curricular Roadmap and Competencies	Curricular Roadmap and Competencies	Curricular Roadmap and Competencies	Curricular Roadmap and Competencies
Month 4					
Month 5					
Month 6					
Month 7					
Month 8					
Month 9					
Month 10					
Month 11					
Month 12	Professional Development Training	Professional Development Training	Professional Development Training	Professional Development Training	Professional Development Training

Appendix B: Self-Reflection on Culturally Responsive and Humble Practices

Self-reflection and self-assessment, particularly related to this content, should be a regular part of your professional experience as a behavior analyst. The following questions are meant to assist you in identifying any potential negative implicit biases that you may hold, along with identifying how many of your practices are consistently culturally responsive and humble. Some of the reflection questions may make you feel uncomfortable, and that is alight. Do your best to be honest and kind to yourself as you explore these topics. It is best to engage with these self-reflection questions under optimal conditions. For example, plan to review them during a time when you are not rushed or overly tired. Consider creating an environment to maximize thoughtful reflection such as playing soft music, making a cup of tea or glass of iced water, and sitting near a window for some natural light. You do not have to complete the entire list of self-reflection items all at once. It is fine to complete the content over a few reflection sessions.

Items for General Self-Reflection

1. I sometimes assume that people have bad intentions based on race, culture, religion, gender identity, sexual preference or other identity variable.
2. I generally assume that others share my values and preferences.
3. I am uncomfortable when people express their emotions around me.
4. I generally spend time with those who share my religious, cultural and racial identity
5. I sometimes fail to recognize my own privilege, power, and advantage compared to others.
6. I can fluently describe my cultural identity to others.
7. I consider my communication style more consistent with:
   a. Low context - often rely on explicit and direct verbal instructions; equal control of conversational exchanges by communication partners; privacy and respect for personal space
   b. High context – often rely on contextual cues and stories to direct behavior; voice tone, facial expressions, and other physical cues; allot differential importance and time to communication partners; and valuing of communal space
8. I regularly seek new experiences to learn about other cultures.
9. I have voluntarily enrolled in a cultural competency and responsiveness training course.
10. I am involved in a community of practice that is dedicated to inclusion and fairness.
11. I do not knowingly engage in behavior that is harassing or demeaning to persons based on their gender identity, gender expression, or gendered preferences, interests, or behaviors.
12. I am committed to TGNC-affirming practices.
13. My behavior analytic practices and professional activities actively challenge power imbalances for marginalized communities.

Items for Self-Reflection Specific to Supervision and Clinical Work

1. I consider any cultural differences with my trainees or clients and ask about culturally important variables (e.g., asking open-ended questions, learning about comfortable communication styles, asking about the conditions for respect and inclusion, asking about the meaning assigned to important events for the trainee or client).

2. I consider the social and economic barriers that might impact a trainee's ability to maximize their fieldwork experiences or a client's ability to receive care.

3. I ask kind, open-ended, forthright questions about culture, identity, or potential differences of my trainees and clients.

4. I develop plans for addressing any significant power differentials that exist in supervisory and client relationships.

5. I identify and address various factors (e.g., cultural and religious, SES, ethnicity, race, sexuality, language barriers, and gender roles) that might impact my relationship with my trainees or clients.

6. I directly talk about privilege and disadvantage with my trainees.

7. I feel comfortable engaging in "skilled dialogues" which involve welcoming, sense-making, appreciating, allowing, joining, and harmonizing.

8. I feel comfortable with trainees and clients expressing emotions in a variety of different ways.

9. I am aware of the religious practices of my trainees and clients, and I try to act in ways that are respectful of their practices.

10. I make space for trainees and clients to name their own identities if they wish.

11. I have considered how my own cultural identities shape my worldview and potentially hinder my connections to trainees and clients.

12. When conducting preference assessments or reinforcer assessments, I include items typically associated with all genders available for all clients.

13. I make sure that the stimuli that I use in training and intervention are culturally and racially anchored and inclusive.

14. I take action to actively address inequalities experienced by my supervisees or clients.

Appendix C: NS Self-Assessments and Workload Assessment (for reference only)

New Supervisor Self-Assessment

Foundational Supervision Skills

Instructions: Rate each of the following supervision and mentorship skills as: 3) proficient, 2) developing, 1) not yet acquired. Mark an asterisk (*) if your repertoire for this skill includes some problematic history and performance aspects (e.g., history of harsh feedback and you sometimes behave the same way when you give feedback).

- Score 3 for *proficient* if you perform the skill accurately and consistently with a little preparation, effort, and only minimal distractors.
- Score 2 for *developing* if you are not yet able to perform the skill consistently and accurately, even under optimal conditions.
- Score 1 for *not yet acquired* if you have not yet the opportunity to learn the skill.

New Supervisor Self-Assessment Foundational Supervision Skills	Score
BACB Supervision Requirements	
1. Describe basic requirements (e.g., frequency of supervision, relevant activities, acceptable modalities, use of group supervision).	
2. Name, describe purpose and how to use, and access required documents and forms.	
3. Describe, create, use, and teach others how to use documentation systems.	
4. Develop a contract and review the contract with a supervisee using an informed consent approach.	
TOTAL:	/12
Purpose of Supervision	
1. Describe the purpose for implementing behavior-analytic supervision (e.g., the benefits and desired outcomes).	
2. Describe the potential risks of ineffective supervision (e.g., poor client outcomes, poor supervisee performance).	
TOTAL:	/6

New Supervisor Self-Assessment Foundational Supervision Skills	Score
Structuring Supervision	
1. Develop a positive rapport.	
2. Schedule and run effective meetings based on LeBlanc & Nosik (2019) checklist.	
3. Establish clear performance expectations for the trainee and supervisee.	
4. Conduct assessments of the supervisee or trainee.	
5. Select supervision goals based on an assessment to improve relevant skills (e.g., BACB Task List, code of ethics).	
TOTAL:	**/15**
Training and Performance Management	
1. Explain the purpose of feedback and discuss preferences for trainee to receive and give feedback.	
2. Use Behavior Skills Training (BST) in teaching supervisees and trainees.	
3. Train personnel to competently perform assessment and intervention procedures.	
4. Use performance monitoring, feedback, and reinforcement systems.	
5. Use a functional assessment approach (e.g., performance diagnostics) and tools (Performance Diagnostic Checklist—Human Services; PDC-HS) to identify variables affecting personnel performance.	
6. Use function-based strategies to improve personnel performance.	
TOTAL:	**/18**
Evaluating the Effects of Supervision	
1. Solicit, review, and respond to feedback from supervises, trainees, and others.	
2. Evaluate the effects of supervision (e.g., on client outcomes, on supervisee repertoires).	
3. Implement changes when needed.	
TOTAL:	**/15**

New Supervisor Self-Assessment Foundational Supervision Skills	Score
Monitoring And Managing Stress and Wellness	
1. Monitor your own stress levels and detect the effects of stress on your supervisory skills and on others.	
2. Engage in appropriate self-care strategies to manage stress (i.e., identify alternative behaviors when you notice you are impacted by stress).	
3. Teach supervisees and trainees to monitor their stress levels and detect effects on others.	
4. Teach supervisees and trainees to engage in appropriate self-care strategies to manage stress.	
TOTAL:	/12

New Supervisor Self-Assessment

Advanced Supervision and Mentor Skills

Instructions: Rate each of the following supervision and mentorship skills as: 3) proficient, 2) developing, 1) not yet acquired. Mark an asterisk (*) if your repertoire for this skill includes some problematic history and performance aspects (e.g., history of harsh feedback and you sometimes behave the same way when you give feedback).

- Score 3 for *proficient* if you perform the skill accurately and consistently with a little preparation, effort, and only minimal distractors.
- Score 2 for *developing* if you are not yet able to perform the skill consistently and accurately, even under optimal conditions.
- Score 1 for *not yet acquired* if you have not yet the opportunity to learn the skill.

New Supervisor Self-Assessment Advanced Supervision and Mentoring Skills	Score
Maintaining Supervision	
1. Establish and continually evaluate the health of bi-directional, collaborative supervisory relationships.	
2. Self-monitor your reactions to various mentees, trainees, and supervisees to detect potential fractures in the relationship.	
3. Ask the supervisee or trainee open-ended questions to produce insight about their own actions, knowledge, and understanding.	
4. Identify and address cultural variables in supervisory relationships.	
5. Identify your own professional reinforcers to foster career sustainability.	
6. Assist your supervisees and trainees to identify their professional reinforcers to foster career sustainability.	
TOTAL:	/18

New Supervisor Self-Assessment Advanced Supervision and Mentoring Skills	Score
Training and Performance Management	
1. Teach supervisees and trainees how to discuss and train feedback delivery and reception skills.	
2. Prepare for and have crucial conversations with your own supervisees, trainees, families, colleagues, and supervisors.	
3. Teach supervisees and trainees to prepare for and have crucial conversations with supervisees, trainees, families, colleagues, and supervisors.	
4. Describe your own performance and the reasons why you performed that way while performing (i.e., a running descriptive narrative while you are behaving).	
5. Teach supervisees and trainees how to self-observe and describe their performance and the reasons for it while performing (i.e., how to use a running narrative to describe why they do what they do).	
6. Teach supervisees and trainees to use Behavioral Training Skills (BST).	
7. Guide supervisees and trainees through structured problem-solving analyses rather than solving problems for them.	
8. Assess and address supervisees' and trainees' organization and time management issues that impact professional performance.	
9. Assess and address supervisees' and trainees' interpersonal skill deficits that impact professional performance.	
TOTAL:	/27
Evaluating the Effects of Supervision	
1. Teach supervisees and trainees to engage in self-evaluation.	
2. Teach supervisees and trainees to solicit and evaluate feedback.	
3. Teach supervisees and trainees to engage in self-monitoring.	
TOTAL:	/9
Monitoring and Managing Stress and Wellness	
1. Create a structured self-monitoring plan to maintain self-care.	
2. Access supports (e.g., colleagues, supervisors/mentors, professionals) to assist in problem solving and managing stress.	
3. Enhance and refine organization and time management (OTM) and problem-solving to decrease stress.	
4. Teach supervisees and trainees to create a structured self-monitoring plan to maintain self-care.	
5. Teach supervisees and trainees to access supports (e.g., colleagues, supervisors/ mentors, professionals) to assist in problem solving and managing stress.	
6. Teach supervisees and trainees to enhance and refine OTM and problem-solving to decrease stress.	
TOTAL:	/18

Workload Assessment

Task	Average Weekly Time Requirement	Facilitators	Barriers
Client caseload management			
RBT caseload			
BCaBA caseload			
Trainee caseload			
Administrative responsibilities			
Other duties			
Total average weekly work hours			

Founded in 1997 by Jose A. Martinez-Diaz, Ph.D. BCBA-D (1950-2020). Women-owned and operated, ABA Technologies specializes in delivering customized instructional design and evidence-based learning solutions to industries of all types. Our approach is rooted in more than 75 years of research in the science of behavior while our momentum is always moving towards the latest in instructional design innovation. We have been established in the learning space for two decades and have developed robust R&D and delivery capabilities, allowing us to scale and customize solutions to meet our customers' individual needs. Our technical capabilities include highly secure online data management and storage, stable website software applications, and web hosting capabilities that offer our customers a seamless and effective learning experience.

abatechnologies.com

 ABA Technologies, Inc.   @abatechnologies   @abatechnologies   @aba_technologies   ABA Technologies, Inc.

ABA Technologies, Inc. Brands

ABA Technologies, Inc. **ABA Tech Academy** **KeyPress Publishing**

Offering professional development programs for continuing education and career or personal growth is one way we support our mission and the field of behavior analysis. We offer a superior level of learner focus and instructional design, high-quality content from leading experts in the field, and easy to use platform that allows for learning anytime and easy connections to other learners.

A Sample of ABA Tech Academy Courses:

"I like the module/phase chunking of the course, the recordings, and the interactive question-answer practice. The instructors were enjoyable to listen to, professional, and knowledgeable. I loved Jose's comments at the end, and the tribute to Jose was beautifully done."

–Stacey, Verified student in the OBM Specialist Certificate course

abatechnologies.com/aba-technologies-academy

We strive to provide individualized services and support to all our authors. Our team of experts is here to answer all your questions and produce your ideal products. We offer personal attention from the time you reach out, through the writing, submission, and review process, close partnerships with our design team to fulfill your visions, and our publishing expertise to help you publish, promote, and sell your book.

A Sample of KeyPress Publications:

"The book KeyPress created for me is professional and beautiful, and we already have another book in process."

–Janis Allen, Owner of Performance Leadership Consulting

keypresspublishing.com

Register your book with KeyPress Publishing

Registered users receive exclusive reader benefits and stay connected with:

- Special discounts on books and ABA Tech Academy courses
- Opportunities to preview new products
- Subscription to ABA Technologies' monthly newsletter that delivers tools, tips, and articles focused on instructional design innovation, BACB ACE CEs, and professional development courses